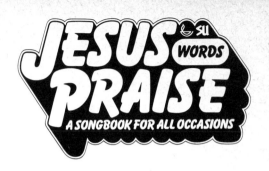

JESUS PRAISE
WORDS
A SONGBOOK FOR ALL OCCASIONS

KU-130-960

© Scripture Union 1982
First published 1982
Reprinted 1982

Compiled by **Norman Warren, David Peacock**
Words arranged by **Michael Perry**
Musical notation checked by **Noel Tredinnick**
Edited by **Simon Jenkins**

Scripture Union, 130 City Road, London EC1V 2NJ

Cover photograph: British Tourist Authority

ISBN 0 85421 962 5

Design and phototypesetting by
Nuprint Services Ltd., Harpenden, Herts.
Printed and bound in Great Britain
at The Pitman Press, Bath

INTRODUCTION

Revival in the church has invariably gone hand in hand with musical expression. Hymns, songs, and the shorter, simpler chorus have been pouring out over the past decade. Dozens of song books have been produced all over the world. Why then another?

In order to have a very good variety of songs and choruses it has often been necessary to have a caseful of books. The aim of **Jesus Praise** has been to gather in one book a wide selection of those songs and choruses that have proved their worth over the past years. As well as this, a third of the book contains new and unpublished material.

Jesus Praise is intended as a replacement for the enormously popular **Youth Praise** books – but it has a wider appeal. It is a book not only for young people, but also adults. It is an all-age Christian songbook. **Jesus Praise** should meet a widely-expressed need for a book of songs and choruses that can be used in public worship, at prayer meetings, in home groups, in youth groups and at family prayers.

The book contains a Scripture Index, so that those who are leading worship will be able to use choruses that relate directly to biblical themes and passages.

All possible effort has been made to trace copyright owners – which is no easy task when many well-known songs have become part and parcel of the life of the average church. Any errors or omissions will gladly be put right at the first opportunity.

It is our hope and prayer that public and home worship will be enriched through this book.

Norman Warren, David Peacock

And I heard every creature in heaven, on earth, in the world below and in the sea – all living creatures in the universe – and they were singing:

To him who sits on the throne and to the Lamb
be praise and honour, glory and might, for ever and ever.

Revelation 5:13

CONTENTS

ACKNOWLEDGEMENTS

This book had its origins in the Youth Praise committee, and many members of that original committee have given much encouragement and valuable advice on the contents of this present book.

We are particularly grateful to Michael Perry for checking all the words and punctuation and to Jean Dean for typing and retyping the words and sending out endless letters.

We thankfully acknowledge the continued help and guidance of our printers. Finally a special thank you to my wife Yvonne, who has had to put up with bits of music lying all over the house for the best part of two years.

Norman Warren

PRAISE AND
THANKSGIVING

1 David Peacock

1 Alleluia, alleluia,
alleluia, alleluia.

2 You are worthy,
you are worthy,
you are worthy
of all our praise.

3 Lord forgive us,
cleanse, remake us.
Lord, remember our
sin no more.

4 Lord we love you,
Lord we love you,
Lord we love you –
we love you Lord.

5 Alleluia, alleluia,
alleluia, alleluia!

*Other verses can be added,
for example: 'Lord we serve you;
Lord we thank you' etc.*

2 Don Fishel

Alleluia, alleluia,
  give thanks to the risen Lord!
Alleluia, alleluia,
  give praise to his name!

1 Jesus is Lord of all the earth,
  he is the king of creation:
    Alleluia, alleluia...

2 Spread the good news through all the earth,
  Jesus has died and has risen:
    Alleluia, alleluia...

3 We have been crucified with Christ –
  now we shall live for ever:
    Alleluia, alleluia...

4 God has proclaimed the just reward –
  life for all men, alleluia!
    Alleluia, alleluia...

5 Come, let us praise the living God,
  joyfully sing to our saviour!
    Alleluia, alleluia...

3 Frank Hernandez

1 Alleluia, alleluia,
   he is Lord, he is Lord;
      alleluia, Jesus is Lord!
   Alleluia, alleluia,
   he is Lord, he is Lord;
      alleluia, Jesus is Lord,
      alleluia, Jesus is Lord!

2 Alleluia, alleluia,
   he is king, he is king;
      alleluia, Jesus is king!
   Alleluia, alleluia,
   he is king, he is king;
      alleluia, Jesus is king,
      alleluia, Jesus is king!

4 Dale Garratt

Alleluia!
   for the Lord our God the almighty reigns;
alleluia!
   for the Lord our God the almighty reigns:
Let us rejoice and be glad
   and give the glory unto him:
Alleluia!
   for the Lord our God the almighty reigns.

5 Unknown

Alleluia! –
  going to sing all about it;
alleluia! –
  going to shout all about it;
alleluia! –
  can't live without it: praise God!

Now I'm living in a new creation,
now I'm drinking at the well of salvation,
now there is no condemnation: praise God!

6 Paul Armstrong

Break forth and sing for joy,
break forth and sing for joy,
break forth and sing for joy and sing praises!

Break forth and sing for joy,
break forth and sing for joy,
break forth and sing for joy and sing praises!

Shout joyfully to the Lord all the earth:
serve the Lord with gladness all the earth!
Come before him with joyful singing:
Know that the Lord himself is God!

Break forth and sing for joy,
break forth and sing for joy,
break forth and sing for joy and sing praises!

7 from Psalm 47
Alan Warren

*Clap your hands all you people,
clap your hands all you people!
Worship the Lord all your days,
trust in the Lord always,
sing to the Lord with shouts of praise:
clap your hands, clap your hands,
Clap your hands...

1 His peace will keep us,
   his life remake us,
   his light will guide us,
   his hands will take us,
   his arms enfold us,
      so, clap your hands,
      Clap your hands...

2 His grace will save us,
   his love refresh us,
   his joy will fill us,
   his truth will teach us,
   his power uplift us,
      so, clap your hands,
      Clap your hands...

* *Clapping ad lib.*

8   from Psalm 47
Jimmy Owens

Clap your hands all you people,
shout unto God with a voice of triumph;
clap your hands all your people,
shout unto God with a voice of praise:
   Hosanna! Hosanna!
Shout unto God with a voice of triumph:
   Praise him! Praise him!
Shout unto God with a voice of praise.

A round

9   Mimi Armstrong Farra

1 Come and bless, come and praise,
  come and praise the living God:
  allelu, allelu, alleluia, Jesus Christ!

    *Allelu, allelu, alleluia, Jesus Christ!
    Allelu, allelu, alleluia, Jesus Christ!

2 Come and hear, come and know,
  come and know the living God:
  allelu, allelu, alleluia, Jesus Christ!
  Allelu...

3 Come and bless, come and praise,
    come and praise the Word of God:
    allelu, allelu, alleluia, Jesus Christ!
        Allelu...

4 Angel choirs sing above,
    'Glory to the Son of God!' –
    joyful Christians sing below
    'Alleluia, Jesus Christ!'
        Allelu...

    * Alternative refrain

    Glory to the Son of God
    Glory to our King
    Glory to our loving Lord
    Glory we will sing.
    Alleluia, Jesus Christ, alleluia,
    Jesus Christ, alleluia, Jesus Christ.

10 A. Carter

1 Come and praise him, Royal Priesthood,
    come and worship, Holy Nation,
    worship Jesus our redeemer;
    he is precious, king of glory!

2 Come and praise him, God's own children,
    come and worship, Chosen People,
    worship Jesus, our redeemer;
    he is precious, king of glory!

11 from Hebrews 12
M. Kerry

Come and praise the living God,
come and worship, come and worship! _
he has made you priest and king:
come and worship the living God!

1 We come not to a mountain of fire and smoke,
   not to gloom or darkness or trumpet sound;
   we come to the new Jerusalem –
   the holy city of God:
   Come and praise...

2 By his voice he shakes the earth,
   his judgements known throughout the world;
   but we have a city that for ever stands –
   the holy city of God:
   Come and praise...

12 from Psalm 134
Unknown

Men: Come, bless the Lord...
Women: Come, bless the Lord...
Men: all you servants of the Lord...
Women: all you servants of the Lord...
Men: who stand by night...
Women: who stand by night...
Men: in the house of the Lord;
Women: in the house of the Lord;

Men:	lift up your hands...
Women:	lift up your hands...
Men:	in the holy place...
Women:	in the holy place...
Men:	and bless the Lord...
Women:	and bless the Lord...
Men:	and bless the Lord!
Women:	and bless the Lord!

13 Unknown

1 Come into his presence singing,
   Alleluia! alleluia! alleluia!
  Come into his presence singing,
   Alleluia!

2 Come into his presence singing,
   Jesus is Lord!...

3 Come into his presence singing,
   Worthy the Lamb!...

4 Come into his presence singing,
   Glory to God!...

5 Come into his presence singing,
   Alleluia!...

14 from Psalm 95
Michael Perry

1 Come, sing praises to the Lord above!
   rock of our salvation, God of love;
   to his presence with thanksgiving move
   for the Lord our God is king:

   He's the king above the mountains high,
   the sea is his, the land and sky –
   subterranean depths that man defy
   are in the hollow of his hand.

2 Here we worship him and bow the knee
   for the shepherd of the flock is he;
   mindful of his generosity,
   sing the praise of God the king!
   He's the king...

3 Hear a salutary story now,
   you with stubborn hearts who will not bow;
   mind his people that rebelled, and how
   he showed them he was their king!
   He's the king...

4 Forty years he kept their prize away,
   made them wander till they walked his way,
   exiled all of them until the day
   they should honour him as king:
   He's the king...

15 Terrye Coleho

1 Father we adore you,
   lay our lives before you:
   how we love you!

2 Jesus we adore you,
   lay our lives before you:
   how we love you!

3 Spirit we adore you,
   lay our lives before you:
   how we love you!

16 Unknown

Glory, praise, and honour
   we bring to him,
the Lord of all creation:
   praise him, praise him!

A round

17 Ron Griffeth

1 Glory to the king, Jesus
  let our praises ring, Jesus
  bless him as we sing! Jesus, Jesus, Jesus

2 Glory to the king, Jesus
  praise his holy name, Jesus
  he is still the same! Jesus, Jesus, Jesus

Women's descant:
Glory, Jesus, glory, Jesus, glory, Jesus, Jesus, Jesus.

18 Jimmy Owens

1 Holy, holy, holy, holy,
  holy, holy, Lord God Almighty! –
  and we lift our hearts before you
  as a token of our love:
  holy, holy, holy, holy!

2 Gracious Father, gracious Father,
  we're so glad to be your children, gracious Father;
  and we lift our heads before you
  as a token of our love,
  gracious Father, gracious Father.

3 Precious Jesus, precious Jesus,
  we're so glad that you've redeemed us, precious Jesus;
  and we lift our hands before you
  as a token of our love,
  precious Jesus, precious Jesus.

JESUS PRAISE

4 Holy Spirit, Holy Spirit,
   come and fill our hearts anew, Holy Spirit! –
   and we lift our voice before you
   as a token of our love,
   Holy Spirit, Holy Spirit.

5 Hallelujah, hallelujah,
   hallelujah, hallelujah! –
   and we lift our hearts before you
   as a token of our love:
   hallelujah, hallelujah!

19 after Revelation 4 and 5
       Unknown

1 Holy, holy, holy is the Lord;
   holy is the Lord God almighty!
   Holy, holy, holy is the Lord;
   holy is the Lord God almighty,
      who was, and is, and is to come:
      holy, holy, holy is the Lord!

2 Jesus, Jesus, Jesus is the Lord;
   Jesus is the Lord God almighty...!

3 Worthy, worthy, worthy is the Lord;
   worthy is the Lord God almighty...!

4 Glory, glory, glory to the Lord;
   glory to the Lord God almighty...!

PRAISE AND THANKSGIVING

20 after Psalm 100
Unknown

I will enter his gates with thanksgiving in my heart,
I will enter his courts with praise;
I will say this is the day that the Lord has made,
 I will rejoice for he has made me glad.

He has made me glad, he has made me glad,
 I will rejoice for he has made me glad.
He has made me glad, he has made me glad,
 I will rejoice for he has made me glad.

21 from John 8, Psalm 126 etc.
Max Dyer

1 I will sing, I will sing a song unto the Lord,
 I will sing, I will sing a song unto the Lord,
 I will sing, I will sing a song unto the Lord:
 Alleluia, glory to the Lord:

 Allelu, alleluia, glory to the Lord,
 allelu, alleluia, glory to the Lord,
 allelu, alleluia, glory to the Lord,
 alleluia, glory to the Lord!

2 We will come, we will come as one before the Lord,...
 alleluia, glory to the Lord!
  Allelu, alleluia...

3 If the Son, if the Son shall make you free,...
you shall be free indeed:
Allelu, alleluia...

4 They that sow in tears shall reap in joy,...
alleluia, glory to the Lord!
Allelu, alleluia...

22   from Psalm 22
Brent Chambers

1 In the presence of your people
    I will praise your name,
for alone you are holy,
    enthroned on the praises of Israel!
Let us celebrate your goodness
    and your steadfast love –
may your name be exalted
    here on earth and in heaven above.

2 Lai – lai – lai...

PRAISE AND THANKSGIVING

23 Unknown

1 The joy of the Lord is my strength,
   the joy of my Lord is my strength,
   the joy of my Lord is my strength,
      the joy of my Lord is my strength!

2 If you want joy, you must sing for it,
   if you want joy, you must sing for it,
   if you want joy, you must sing for it:
      the joy of the Lord is my strength!

3 If you want joy, you must shout for it,
   if you want joy, you must shout for it,
   if you want joy, you must shout for it:
      the joy of the Lord is my strength!

4 If you want joy, you must jump for it,
   if you want joy, you must jump for it,
   if you want joy, you must jump for it:
      the joy of the Lord is my strength!

24 Unknown

1 Ju–bi–late Deo, jubilate Deo, alleluia!
2   Ju –bi – late ...
3   Ju –bi – late ...

A round

JESUS PRAISE

25 from Psalm 100
Michael Perry

1 Jubilate everybody,
  serve the Lord with gladness;
  O be joyful everybody
  come before him singing:
      Come into his church with praise,
      come in through those doors to thank him!

2 Know that he, the God who made us,
  he it is who owns us;
  we, the people of his care,
  the sheep upon his hillside:
      Come into his church with praise,
      come in through those doors to thank him!

3 For the Lord our God is good –
  his love is everlasting;
  and his faithfulness endures
  to every generation:
      Come into his church with praise
      come in through those doors to thank him!

  Jubilate everybody.
  Jubilate De-o!

26 from Psalm 95
Norman Warren

1 Let us come into his presence,
  the Lord of heaven and earth! –
  let us sing to him with triumph,
  our rock, our saviour, friend:

> *All glory, praise and honour,*
> *be his for evermore –*
> *let us come into his presence,*
> *the Lord of heaven and earth.*

2 Let us come before him with thanksgiving,
  and sing to him with psalms:
  he is king above all creation,
  the Lord is a mighty God:
    All glory...

3 In his hand the depths of the earth,
  the mountain peaks are his;
  the sea is his and he made it –
  he formed the dry land:
    All glory...

4 Let us kneel before our maker
  for he himself is our God! –
  we are the people of his pasture,
  the sheep of his hand:
    All glory...

5 All glory to the Father,
    all glory to the Son,
    all glory to the Holy Spirit,
    for evermore! Amen:
        All glory...

27 from Psalm 95
        Norman Warren

1 Let us praise the Lord our God,
    come before him, shout his praises:
    let us sing with thankful hearts,
    come before him full of joy!
        Every throne must bow to him,
        he is Lord of everything:
        praise our maker, praise our saviour,
        praise the Lord our king!

2 In his hands he holds the earth,
    mountains high and oceans deep;
    every valley every hill,
    all creation they are his:
        Every throne must bow to him,
        he is Lord of everything:
        praise our maker, praise our saviour,
        praise the Lord our king!

3 This great God is our God –
　　let us kneel to him who made us;
　　shepherd of the flock is he,
　　he will guide us with his hand:
　　　　Every throne must bow to him,
　　　　he is Lord of everything:
　　　　praise our maker, praise our saviour,
　　　　praise the Lord our King!

　　Praise our maker, praise our saviour,
　　praise the Lord our king!

28 from Luke 1
Michael Perry

1 Mary sang a song, a song of love,
　　magnified the mighty Lord above;
　　melodies of praise his name extol
　　from the very depths of Mary's soul:

2 'God the Lord has done great things for me,
　　looked upon my life's humility;
　　happy, they shall call me from this day –
　　merciful is he whom we obey.

3 'To the humble soul our God is kind,
　　to the proud he brings unease of mind:
　　who uplifts the poor, pulls down the strong? –
　　God alone has power to right the wrong.

4 'He who has been Israel's strength and stay
fills the hungry, sends the rich away;
he has shown his promise firm and sure
faithful to his people evermore.'

5 This was Mary's song as we recall,
mother to the saviour of us all:
magnify his name and sing his praise
worship and adore him all your days!

29 after Psalm 136
Unknown

1 ¹O give thanks, O give thanks,
O give thanks unto the Lord!
for he is gracious and his ²mercy endures,
endures for ever.

2 ¹Sing to him, sing to him,
sing a new song to the Lord!
for he is gracious and his ²mercy endures,
endures for ever.

3 ¹Worship him, worship him,
come and worship our great God!
for he is gracious and his ²mercy endures,
endures for ever.

2 part round
second part begins at ²

O how good is the Lord,
O how good is the Lord,
O how good is the Lord,
I never will forget what he has done for me!

1 He gives me salvation, how good is the Lord,
  he gives me salvation, how good is the Lord,
  he gives me salvation, how good is the Lord;
  I never will forget what he has done for me:
    O how good..!

2 He gives me his blessings...
    O how good..!

3 He gives me his Spirit...
    O how good..!

4 He gives me his healing...
    O how good..!

5 He gives me his glory...
    O how good..!

31
from Psalm 149
Norman Warren

O praise the Lord, O praise the Lord,
sing to the Lord a new song;
O praise the Lord, O praise the Lord,
sing out his praises all people of God!

1 Let us praise him in the dance,
   let us praise him on the strings,
   let us all be joyful in our king:
       O praise the Lord...

2 Victory belongs to him,
   justice, mercy, truth are his,
   for the Lord takes pleasure in his people:
       O praise the Lord...

32
33
The Doxology
after Thomas Ken and others, Jubilate Hymns version

Praise God from whom all blessings flow,
in heaven above and earth below;
one God, three persons, we adore –
to him be praise for evermore!

PRAISE AND THANKSGIVING

from Psalm 150
Norman Warren

1 Praise the Lord in his holiness,
   praise him for his mighty power,
   praise him in the highest heaven,
   praise him, people here on earth!

2 Let the trumpets sing his glory,
   let the strings resound in praise,
   drum and cymbal crash in harmony,
   praise him, people here on earth!

3 Praise him with the sound of music,
   let the whole world sing with joy,
   every living creature praise him,
   praise the mighty Lord!

4 Glory to the heavenly Father,
   glory to the royal Son,
   glory to the Holy Spirit –
   praise him, praise our God!

35 from Psalm 146
Norman Warren

1 Praise the Lord, praise the Lord my soul! –
  I'll praise the Lord as long as I live:

  And I will sing a song,
  sing a song, sing a song to him;
  a song of praise to my God all my life.

2 Happy the man with the Lord to help him;
  happy the man who depends on the Lord:
    And I will sing...

3 The Lord is king, he is king for evermore;
  the Lord is king, he will reign for all time:
    And I will sing...

36 Jim Stipech

1 Praise you Father! –
  bless you Jesus! –
  Holy Spirit, thank you
  for being here, being here!

2 Praise you Father! –
  bless you Jesus! –
  Holy Spirit thank you
  for being here, being here, Lord!

PRAISE AND THANKSGIVING

37   after Isaiah 40
Mary Smail

1 Prepare the way of the Lord! –
  make his paths straight;
  open the gates that he may enter freely
  into our lives:
  Hosanna! we cry to the Lord.

  *And we will fill the earth
  with the sound of his praise –
  Jesus is Lord! let him be adored!
  Yes, we will have this man to reign over us,
  hosanna! we follow the Lord.*

2 And he will come to us as he came before,
  clothed in his glory, to stand in our place;
  and we behold him, now our priest, Lord and king:
  Hosanna! we sing to the Lord.
  And we will . . .

3 Prepare the way of the Lord!
  make his paths straight;
  open the gates that he may enter freely
  into our lives:
  Hosanna! we cry to the Lord.
  And we will . . .

38 from Philippians 4
Unknown

Rejoice in the Lord always, and again I say rejoice! –
rejoice in the Lord always, and again I say rejoice! –
rejoice, rejoice, and again I say rejoice! –
rejoice, rejoice, and again I say rejoice!

39 from Psalm 98
Timothy Dudley-Smith

1 Sing a new song to the Lord,
   he to whom wonders belong;
   rejoice in his triumph and tell of his power –
   O sing to the Lord a new song!

2 Now to the ends of the earth
   see his salvation is shown;
   and still he remembers his mercy and truth,
   unchanging in love to his own.

3 Sing a new song and rejoice,
   publish his praises abroad;
   let voices in chorus, with trumpet and horn,
   resound for the joy of the Lord!

4 Join with the hills and the sea,
   thunders of praise to prolong;
   in judgement and justice he comes to the earth –
   O sing to the Lord a new song!

PRAISE AND THANKSGIVING

40 Unknown

1 Sing and rejoice, sing and rejoice –
   Jesus is risen: come, lift up your voice!

2 Heaven's praises ring, heaven's praises ring –
   Jesus is risen: to him we will sing.

3 Your voices raise, your voices raise –
   Jesus has saved us: come, give him due praise!

A round

41 M. Cox

Sing his praises! –
heaven raises
    songs of him who died for me;
his the glory,
mine the story
    of the love which sets me free;
love which never will deceive me,
love which never lets me go:
who can measure
half the treasure
    of his love, who loves me so!

42 from Luke 1
Fred Kaan

1 Sing we a song of high revolt –
   make great the Lord, his name exalt:
   sing we the song that Mary sang,
   of God at war with human wrong.

2 Sing we of him who deeply cares,
   and still with us our burden bears;
   he who with strength the proud disowns,
   brings down the mighty from their thrones.

3 By him the poor are lifted up –
   he satisfies with bread and cup
   the hungry men of many lands;
   the rich must go with empty hands.

4 He calls us to revolt and fight
   with him for what is just and right;
   to sing and live Magnificat
   in crowded street and council flat.

43 Chuck Girard

Sometimes 'Alleluia!',
sometimes 'Praise the Lord!',
sometimes gently singing,
our hearts in one accord.

1 O let us lift our voices,
   look toward the sky and start to sing;
   O let us now return his love –
   just let our voices ring!
      Sometimes 'Alleluia!'...

2 O let us feel his presence,
   let the sound of praises fill the air;
   O let us sing the song of Jesus' love,
   to people everywhere!
      Sometimes 'Alleluia!'...

3 O let our joy be unconfined –
   let us sing with freedom unrestrained;
   let's take this feeling that we feel now,
   outside these walls and let it ring!
      Sometimes 'Alleluia!'...

4 O let the Spirit overflow,
   as we are filled from head to toe:
   we love you Father, Son and Spirit,
   and we want the world to know!
      Sometimes 'Alleluia!'...

44 Roger Dyer

Stand up, clap hands, shout: Thank you, Lord,
thank you for the world I'm in!
Stand up, clap hands, shout: Thank you Lord
for happiness and peace within!

1 I look around and the sun's in the sky
   I look around and then I think: Oh my! –
   the world is such a wonderful place,
   and all because of the good Lord's grace.
       Stand up, clap hands...

2 I look around and the creatures I see,
   I look around and it amazes me
   that every fox and bird and hare
   must fit in a special place somewhere.
       Stand up, clap hands...

3 I look around at all the joy I've had,
   I look around and then it makes me glad
   that I can offer thanks and praise,
   to him who guides me through my days.
       Stand up, clap hands...

PRAISE AND THANKSGIVING

45 from Jeremiah 31
Merla Watson

Then shall the young girls rejoice in the dance,
the young men and old men together:
  *Li, li, li ... li, li, li.

Then I shall turn their mourning into joy;
then I will comfort them
and make them rejoice,
  rejoice from their sorrow;
and make them rejoice,
  rejoice in the Lord.

*Li (=his), pronounced 'lie'

46 from Isaiah 51
Ruth Lake

1 Therefore the redeemed of the Lord shall return
  and come with singing unto Zion,
  and everlasting joy shall be upon their head.

2 Therefore the redeemed of the Lord shall return
  and come with singing unto Zion,
  and everlasting joy shall be upon their head.

  They shall obtain gladness and joy
  and sorrow and mourning shall flee away:

3 Therefore the redeemed of the Lord shall return
  and come with singing unto Zion,
  and everlasting joy shall be upon their head.

47 _{Fountain Trust}

1 Therefore we lift our hearts in praise,
  sing to the living God who saves,
  for grace poured out for you and me.

2 There for everyone to see,
  there on the hill at Calvary
  Jesus died for you and me.

3 There for sad and broken men
  he rose up from the grave again,
  and reigns on high for you and me.

4 There for such great pain and cost
  the Spirit came at Pentecost
  and comes in power for you and me.

5 Therefore we lift our hearts in praise,
  sing to the living God who saves,
  for grace poured out for you and me.

They say he's wonderful,
they say he's wonderful;
the sun, the moon, the stars that shine,
the sun, the moon, the stars that shine
say God is wonderful:

1 He makes the rain to fall,
  he sees the wheat grow tall,
  the harvest of the land and sea,
  the harvest of the land and sea,
  in love he gives it all.
  They say he's wonderful...

2 When I see babies small,
  and I hear children call,
  and think of family life and fun,
  and think of family life and fun,
  I know he's behind it all.
  They say he's wonderful...

3 The love men have for him –
  such love death cannot dim,
  of small and great of rich and poor,
  of small and great of rich and poor –
  love like this comes from him.
  They say he's wonderful...

4 And I know he's wonderful,
   I know he's wonderful;
   the Son of God who died for me
   the Son of God who died for me –
   I know he's wonderful.
      They say he's wonderful...

49   Andrae Crouch

1 To God be the glory,
   to God be the glory,
   to God be the glory
   for the things he has done!
      With his blood he has saved me,
      with his power he has raised me:
      to God be the glory for the things he has done!

2 Just let me live my life,
   let it be pleasing Lord to you;
   and if I gain any praise,
   let it go to Calvary.
      With his blood he has saved me,
      with his power he has raised me:
      to God be the glory for the things he has done!

50 Mimi Armstrong Farra

We cry hosanna, Lord;
yes, hosanna, Lord;
yes, hosanna, Lord, to you!

We cry hosanna, Lord;
yes, hosanna, Lord;
yes, hosanna, Lord, to you!

1 Behold, our saviour comes!
  Behold the Son of our God:
  he offers himself and he comes among us,
  a lowly servant to all.
     We cry hosanna...

2 Children wave their palms
  as the King of all kings rides by:
  should we forget to praise our God,
  the very stones would sing.
     We cry hosanna...

3 He comes to set us free,
  he gives us liberty;
  his victory over death
  is the eternal sign
  of God's love for us,
     We cry hosanna...

51 Pam Hansford

We magnify your name, Lord;
we worship and adore you
for who you are,
for what you've done among your people here:
we open up our lives to you,
lay down our minds and wills;
we want you Lord to have your way,
for we delight in you.

52 Unknown

Wherever I am I'll praise him,
whenever I can I'll praise him;
for his love surrounds me like a sea:
   I'll praise the name of Jesus,
   lift up the name of Jesus –
for the name of Jesus lifted me.

53 from Psalm 63
Hugh Mitchell

1 Your loving-kindness is better than life,
  your loving-kindness is better than life –
  my lips shall praise you:
    So will I bless you –
    I will lift up my hands in your name.

2 I lift my hands up in your name,
  I lift my hands up in your name –
  my lips shall praise you:
    So will I bless you –
    I will lift up my hands in your name.

THE FATHER

54 David Bilbrough

Abba, Father, let me be
yours and yours alone;
may my will for ever be,
evermore your own.
Never let my heart grow cold,
never let me go:
Abba, Father, let me be
yours and yours alone!

55 Tim Cullen

Alleluia, my Father, for giving us your Son;
sending him into the world to be given up for men,
knowing we would bruise him and smite him
   from the earth:
alleluia, my Father, in his death is my birth;
alleluia, my Father, in his life is my life.

56 Unknown

1 God is so good,
  God is so good,
  God is so good:
    he's so good to me.

2 He took my sin,
  he took my sin,
  he took my sin:
    he's so good to me.

3 Now I am free,
  now I am free,
  now I am free:
    he's so good to me.

4 God is so good,
  he took my sin,
  now I am free:
    he's so good to me.

57 from Isaiah 6
        Norman Warren

*Holy, holy, holy, the Lord God is holy;
his glory fills the world!*

1 Touch me with the coal of fire;
  touch me with the coal of fire,
  and purge away my sin:
    Holy, holy, holy...

2 Give me, Lord, the word of God;
  give me, Lord, the word of God,
  for here I am, send me!
    Holy, holy, holy...

58 Unknown

How great is our God, how great is his name! –
he's the greatest one, for ever the same:
he rolled back the waters of the mighty Red Sea,
and he said: I'm going to lead you,
    put your trust in me!

59 from Psalm 89
Karen Barrie

1 I have made a covenant with my chosen,
  given my servant my word,
I have made your name to last for ever –
built to outlast all time.

    I will celebrate your love for ever, Yahweh;
    age on age my words proclaim your love,
    for I claim that love is built to last for ever,
    founded firm, your faithfulness.

2 Yahweh, the assembly of those who love you
  applaud your marvellous word:
who in the skies can compare with Yahweh,
who can rival him?
    I will celebrate your love...

3 Happy the people who learn to acclaim you,
  they rejoice in your light:
you are our glory and you are our courage,
our hope belongs to you.
    I will celebrate your love...

THE FATHER

4 I have revealed my chosen servant,
   and he can rely on me;
   giving him my love to last for ever,
   he shall rise in my name.
      I will celebrate your love...

5 He will call to me, my father, my God,
   for I make him my first-born Son;
   I cannot take back my given promise
   I've called him to shine like the sun.
      I will celebrate your love...

60 Dave Rios

I'm in my Father,
and my Father's in me;
the Son and the Spirit
are all living in me.

I'm in my Father,
and my Father's in me;
the Son and the Spirit
are all living in me.

And I'm living in them
because I've been born again;
the blessed Trinity
has called me to their unity.
   I'm in my Father...

61 from Psalm 68
E. Bacon

Let God arise, his enemies be scattered,
let God arise, his enemies be scattered,
let God arise, his enemies be scattered,
let God, let God arise!

62 Unknown

My God is so great, so strong, so mighty,
there's nothing that he cannot do.
My God is so great, so strong, so mighty
there is nothing he cannot do!

The rivers are his, the mountains are his,
the stars are his handiwork too.

My God is so great, so strong, so mighty
there's nothing that he cannot do!

63 from Isaiah 6
Unknown

We see the Lord, we see the Lord,
and he is high and lifted up,
and his train fills the temple;
he is high and lifted up,
and his train fills the temple:
    the angels cry, 'Holy'
    the angels cry, 'Holy',
    the angels cry, 'Holy is the Lord!'

THE FATHER

64   Johnny Lange, Hy Heath and Sonny Burke

1. Who made the mountain, who made the trees,
   who made the river flow to the sea,
   and who hung the moon in the starry sky? –
   somebody bigger than you and I.

2 Who made the flowers bloom in the spring,
   who writes the song for the robin to sing,
   and who sends the rain when the earth is dry? –
   somebody bigger than you and I.

3 He lights the way when the road is long,
   keeps you company; with love to guide you
   he walks beside you, just like he walks with me:

4 When I am weary filled with despair,
   who gives me courage to go on from there?
   And who gives me faith that will never die? –
   somebody bigger than you and I!

THE LORD JESUS CHRIST

65

M. Wilkinson

1 All the way, all the way,
   he came all the way for me;
   all the way, all the way,
   he came all the way for me.

2 From heaven above to Bethlehem
   he came all the way for me...

3 From Bethlehem to Jerusalem
   he came all the way for me...

4 From Jerusalem to Calvary
   he came all the way for me...

5 From Calvary to heaven above
   he came all the way for me...

6 From heaven above into my heart
   he came all the way for me...

7 Jesus came, Jesus came,
   he came all the way for me...

THE LORD JESUS CHRIST

Come and praise the Lord our king, alleluia
come and praise the Lord our king! alleluia

1 Christ was born in Bethlehem, alleluia
  Son of God and Son of Man: alleluia
  Come and praise...

2 He grew up an earthly child, alleluia
  of the world, but undefiled, alleluia
  Come and praise...

3 Jesus died at Calvary, alleluia
  rose again triumphantly! alleluia
  Come and praise...

4 He will cleanse us from our sin, alleluia
  if we live by faith in him: alleluia
  Come and praise...

5 We will live with him one day, alleluia
  and for ever with him stay: alleluia
  Come and praise...

67 Michael Perry

1 Comes Mary to the grave:
   no singing bird has spoken,
   nor has the world awoken,
   and in her grief all love lies lost
      and broken.

2 Says Jesus at her side,
   no longer Jesus dying,
   'Why Mary, are you crying?'
   She turns, with joy, 'My Lord! my love!'
      replying.

3 With Mary on this day
   we join our voices praising
   the God of Jesus' raising,
   and sing the triumph of his love
      amazing.

68 from Isaiah 7
         Geoff Buchan

Emmanuel, Emmanuel,
his name is called Emmanuel –
God with us,
revealed in us –
his name is called Emmanuel.

69 J. Cothram

1 Glorious in majesty, holy in his praises,
Jesus, our saviour, and our king;
born a man, yet God of old:
let us all adore him,
filled with his Spirit let us sing!

Living is to love him,
serving him to know his freedom:
come along with us to join the praise of Jesus,
come to Jesus now, go to live his word rejoicing,
come to Jesus now, go to live his word rejoicing.

2 Victory he won for us,
freeing us from darkness,
dying and rising from the dead:
living with the Father now,
yet he is among us;
we are the body, he the head.
Living is to love him...

3 Brethren, we live in love,
living with each other;
gladly we share each other's pain;
yet he will not leave us so –
soon he is returning,
taking us back with him to reign.
Living is to love him...

70   from Philippians 2
Unknown

He is Lord, he is Lord,
he is risen from the dead, and he is Lord!
Every knee shall bow,
every tongue confess
that Jesus Christ is Lord.

71   from John 14
Keith Routledge

1 He is my saviour and my friend
   and I live my life for him;
   he's all I need from day to day –
   he is the truth, the life, the way.

2 When you give yourself to him,
   he makes everything worthwhile;
   he'll be all you need from day to day –
   he is the truth, the life, the way.

3 Why don't you let him be your friend
   and your saviour and your God?
   He's all you need from day to day –
   he is the truth, the truth, the life, the way.

THE LORD JESUS CHRIST

72   from John 14
Gordon Brattle

1 He is the way – the end of all my searching;
  he is the truth – I'll trust his every word;
  he is the life abundant, everlasting:
  this is the Christ, the saviour of the world!

2 More of the way – dear Lord, be this my choosing;
  more of the truth – Lord, teach me day by day;
  more of the life – for ever satisfying:
  more of yourself – the life, the truth, the way!

73   N. J. Clayton

Higher than the hills, deeper than the sea,
broader than the skies above
is my redeemer's love for me:
to his cross of shame, Jesus freely came,
bearing all my sin and sorrow – wondrous love!

74   from Isaiah 9
Unknown

His name is higher than any other,
his name is Jesus, his name is Lord;
    his name is higher than any other,
    his name is Jesus, his name is Lord.
His name is Wonderful, his name is Counsellor,
his name is Prince of peace, the mighty God;
    his name is higher than any other,
    his name is Jesus, his name is Lord.

JESUS PRAISE

75 Unknown

His name is Wonderful, his name is Wonderful,
    his name is Wonderful, Jesus my Lord;
he is the mighty king, master of everything,
    his name is Wonderful, Jesus my Lord!

He's the great shepherd, the rock of all ages,
    almighty God is he;
bow down before him, love and adore him,
    his name is Wonderful, Jesus my Lord!

76 from Isaiah 52
Lenny Smith

How lovely on the mountains are the feet of him
who brings good news, good news! –
announcing peace, proclaiming news of happiness:
    Our God reigns, our God reigns, our God reigns,
    our God reigns, our God reigns, our God reigns!

Alternative Version (from Isaiah 52, 53)

1 How lovely on the mountains are the feet of him
  who brings good news, good news;
  announcing peace, proclaiming news of happiness,
  saying to Zion: Your God reigns!
    Your God reigns, your God reigns,
    your God reigns, your God reigns!

THE LORD JESUS CHRIST

2 He had no stately form, he had no majesty,
  that we should be drawn to him;
  he was despised and we took no account of him,
  yet now he reigns with the Most High:
    Now he reigns, now he reigns,
    now he reigns with the Most High!

3 It was our sin and guilt that bruised and wounded him;
  it was our sin that brought him down:
  when we like sheep had gone astray, our shepherd came,
  and on his shoulders bore our shame:
    On his shoulders, on his shoulders,
    on his shoulders he bore our shame.

4 Meek as a lamb that's led out to the slaughterhouse,
  dumb as a sheep before its shearer,
  his life ran down upon the ground like pouring rain,
  that we might be born again:
    That we might be, that we might be
    that we might be born again.

5 Out from the tomb he came with grace and majesty:
  he is alive, he is alive!
  God loves us so – see here his hands, his feet, his side!
  Yes, we know, he is alive:
    He is alive, he is alive
    he is alive, he is alive!

6 How lovely on the mountains are the feet of him
  who brings good news, good news;
  announcing peace, proclaiming news of happiness:
  Our God reigns, our God reigns!
    Our God reigns, our God reigns,
    our God reigns, our God reigns!

77
from John 6
S. Suzanne Toolan

1 I am the bread of life:
   he who comes to me shall not hunger,
   he who believes in me shall not thirst;
   no-one can come to me unless the Father draw him:

   And I will raise him up, and I will raise him up,
   and I will raise him up on the last day.

2 The bread that I will give,
   is my flesh for the life of the world,
   and he who eats of this bread, he shall live for ever,
   he shall live for ever:
       And I will raise him up . . .

3 Unless you eat of the flesh of the Son of Man
   and drink of his blood, and drink of his blood,
   you shall not have life within you:
       And I will raise him up . . .

4 I am the resurrection, I am the life;
   he who believes in me, even if he die,
   he shall live for ever:
       And I will raise him up . . .

5 Yes Lord, we believe
   that you are the Christ, the Son of God
   who has come into the world:

       And you will raise us up, and you will raise us up,
       and you will raise us up on the last day.

THE LORD JESUS CHRIST

78 Unknown

In the name of Jesus, in the name of Jesus
    we have the victory;
in the name of Jesus, in the name of Jesus,
    Satan will have to flee.
Who can tell what God can do;
    who can tell of his love for you?
In the name of Jesus, Jesus,
    we have the victory.

79 Unknown (18th century)

1 Jesus Christ is risen today, alleluia
    our triumphant holy day; alleluia
    who did once upon the cross
    suffer to redeem our loss: alleluia

2 Hymns of praise then let us sing, alleluia
    now to Christ our heavenly king! – alleluia
    who endured the cross and grave
    sinners to redeem and save: alleluia

3 But the pains which he endured, alleluia
    our salvation have procured; alleluia
    now beyond the sky he's king
    where the angels ever sing: alleluia

80 Margaret Bowdler

1 Jesus Christ, one with God,
    you are Lord of all:
in this vast universe
    man seems very small.
Can it be, he whose works
    all the heavens span,
can look down lovingly –
    care for mere man?

2 Love of God, shown to man
    by his only Son:
through his life and his death
    our salvation won.
Love of God fill my life
    that I may serve you,
telling all of the love
    shown on Calvary!

3 Peace of God, passing all
    man can comprehend,
fill my heart, calm my fears,
    keep me to the end!
Fear and strife, war and want
    all around I see:
only Christ, prince of peace,
    brings tranquility.

Jesus Christ, lead me on
    to eternity . . .
to eternity!

THE LORD JESUS CHRIST

81 Dave Bolton

Jesus, how lovely you are!
You are so gentle, so pure and kind,
you shine like the morning star:
Jesus how lovely you are!

1 Alleluia, Jesus is my Lord and king;
alleluia, Jesus is my everything.
   Jesus, how lovely you are...!

2 Alleluia, Jesus died and rose again;
alleluia, Jesus forgave all my sin.
   Jesus, how lovely you are...!

3 Alleluia, Jesus is meek and lowly;
alleluia, Jesus is pure and holy.
   Jesus, how lovely you are...!

4 Alleluia, Jesus is the bridegroom;
alleluia, Jesus will take his bride soon.
   Jesus, how lovely you are...!

82 Norman Warren

1 Jesus I worship you,
  Jesus I worship you,
  Jesus I worship you,
  Son of God:
      You came from heaven above
      to bring the Father's love
      Jesus I worship you,
      Son of God!

2 Jesus I trust in you,
  Jesus I trust in you,
  Jesus I trust in you,
  Son of God:
      You died on Calvary
      to set my Spirit free.
      Jesus I trust in you,
      Son of God!

3 Jesus I feed on you,
  Jesus I feed on you,
  Jesus I feed on you,
  Son of God:
      You are the living bread,
      you meet my every need,
      Jesus I feed on you,
      Son of God!

THE LORD JESUS CHRIST

4 Jesus I love you,
  Jesus I love you,
  Jesus I love you,
  Son of God:
    I give my self to you,
    lay down my life for you,
    Jesus I love you,
    Son of God!

83 Philip Moore

Jesus is Lord, Jesus is Lord,
alleluia!
Jesus is Lord, Jesus is Lord,
alleluia!
  Alleluia, alleluia,
  alleluia, alleluia!

This may be sung as a round

84 Alan Durden

1 Jesus is the name we worship,
  Jesus is the friend we love
  Jesus is our Lord and saviour,
  king of heaven above.

2 Jesus knows when we are troubled,
  Jesus hears our every prayer,
  Jesus has our trials and sorrows
  always in his care.

3 Jesus made the lame go walking,
  Jesus made the blind to see,
  Jesus healed the sick and wounded:
  wondrous, O was he!

4 Jesus is our great redeemer,
  Jesus died for you and me,
  Jesus took our sins and failings,
  bore them on the Tree.

5 Jesus lives within us daily,
  Jesus in our hearts will stay
  till we meet with him in heaven
  on that glorious day.

THE LORD JESUS CHRIST

85 A. Paget Wilkes

1 Jesus, Jesus, Jesus!
   sweetest name on earth:
   how can I, a sinner,
   come to know its worth?

2 O the sinful sorrow,
   O the strangest shame,
   that I saw no beauty
   in that sacred name:

3 Never found the mystery
   in that simple word,
   Jesus, Jesus, Jesus –
   saviour, friend and Lord!

4 Jesus, Jesus, Jesus!
   loved me in my shame:
   O the joy and wonder
   in that sacred name!

86 Unknown

Jesus, Jesus, Jesus,
your love has melted my heart;
Jesus, Jesus, Jesus,
your love has melted my heart!

87 Unknown

Jesus, Jesus,
let me tell you what I know! –
you have given us your *Spirit;
we love you so.
*Or 'life', 'love', 'glory', 'riches' . . .

88 Unknown

*Jesus' love is very wonderful,
Jesus' love is very wonderful,
Jesus' love is very wonderful –
O wonderful love!*

So high, you can't get over it,
so low, you can't get under it,
so wide, you can't get round it –
O wonderful love!

*Jesus' love is very wonderful,
Jesus' love is very wonderful,
Jesus' love is very wonderful –
O wonderful love!*

Or 'Love of God – O how wonderful!'

89 Robert Stoodley

Jesus, my saviour, O how I love you,
for you have filled me with your new life;
all your heavenly glory you counted as nothing
and bore the pain of death to make us free:

Therefore with all my heart I'll gladly sing your praise
and do so all my days to bless your holy name,
for God has exalted you, seated at the Father's side:
you shall be glorified, Jesus our king:

Therefore with all my heart I'll gladly sing your praise
and do so all my days to bless your holy name,
for God has exalted you, seated at the Father's side:
you shall be glorified, Jesus our king!

90 Naida Hearn

1 Jesus, name above all names,
   beautiful saviour, glorious Lord,
   Emmanuel – God is with us!
   blessed redeemer, living Word.

2 Jesus, bearer of my sins,
   beautiful saviour, glorious Lord,
   you suffered giving me freedom:
   living redeemer, you are my Lord!

3 Jesus, name above all names,
  suffering servant, faithful friend
  good shepherd, risen master,
  king of glory, Lord of all!

91

Unknown

1 Joy of Jesus, grows and grows,
  joy of Jesus, overflows,
  joy of Jesus, makes my spirit free:
  thank you, Lord, for giving it to me!

2 Love of Jesus, grows and grows,
  love of Jesus, overflows,
  love of Jesus, makes my spirit free:
  thank you, Lord, for giving it to me!

3 Peace of Jesus, grows and grows,
  peace of Jesus, overflows,
  peace of Jesus, makes my spirit free:
  thank you, Lord, for giving it to me.

92 Keith Routledge

1 Just one touch of his hand
   and you will understand
   what Jesus can do for you:
       Just one look from his eyes
       and you will realize
       what Jesus can do for you.

2 Just one word – it's his voice you heard –
   then you'll know peace of mind
   with Jesus in your heart:
       Just one touch of his hand
       and you will understand
       what Jesus can do for you –
       what Jesus can do for you.

93 after Song of Solomon 2
Paul Goodwin

Lord Jesus, Lord Jesus, what a wonder you are! –
you are brighter than the morning star,
you are fairer – much fairer –
than the lilies that grow by the wayside;
precious, more precious than gold.

1 You're like the rose of Sharon,
   the fairest of the fair;
   you are all my heart could ever desire:
   Lord Jesus, Lord Jesus what a wonder you are! –
   you are precious, more precious than gold.
       Lord Jesus, Lord Jesus . . . !

2 You are the king of glory, the sun of righteousness,
   and your beauty shines upon our lives:
   Lord Jesus, Lord Jesus what a wonder you are! –
   you are precious, more precious than gold.

94   Laura Winnen

My Lord, he is a-coming soon –
prepare the way of the Lord!
Get everything ready for that day:
prepare the way of the Lord!

1 If you're asleep, it's time to wake up:
   awake, O sleeper, arise!
   If you're in the dark, it's time to be lit:
   awake, O sleeper, arise!
   My Lord, he is a-coming...

2 Come, Lord Jesus, come into my heart:
   prepare the way of the king!
   He is coming, he's coming soon:
   prepare the way of the king!
   My Lord, he is a-coming...

95 after John 14
Keith Routledge

1 My peace I give unto you:
   it's a peace that the world cannot give,
   it's a peace that the world cannot understand;
   peace to know, peace to live –
   my peace I give unto you.

2 My joy I give unto you:
   it's a joy that the world cannot give,
   it's a joy that the world cannot understand;
   joy to know, joy to live –
   my joy I give unto you.

3 My love I give unto you:
   it's a love that the world cannot give,
   it's a love that the world cannot understand;
   love to know, love to live –
   my love I give unto you.

96 Keith Routledge

   Nothing but the *love of Jesus –
   we have to sing about it;
   nothing but the *love of Jesus –
   we have to talk about it!
   Nothing but the *love of Jesus
   is changing the way we live;
   nothing but the *love of Jesus,
   His good news of peace and joy –
   that's all we've got to give.

JESUS PRAISE

Do you know, do you know him?
Do you love, do you love him?

Or 'power', etc.

97
J. M. C. Crum

1 Now the green blade rises from the buried grain –
   wheat that in the dark earth many days has lain:
   Love lives again, that with the dead has been,
   Love is come again, like wheat that springs green.

2 In the grave they laid him, Love whom men had slain,
   thinking that never he would wake again;
   laid in the earth like grain that sleeps unseen –
   Love is come again, like wheat that springs green.

3 Forth he came at Easter, like the risen grain,
   he that for three days in the grave had lain;
   live from the dead my risen Lord is seen –
   Love is come again, like wheat that springs green.

4 When our hearts are wintry, grieving or in pain,
   your touch can call us back to life again;
   fields of our hearts that dead and bare have been –
   Love is come again, like wheat that springs green.

98 Unknown

1 O the blood of Jesus,
   O the blood of Jesus,
   O the blood of Jesus,
   it washes white as snow!

2 O the word of Jesus,
   O the word of Jesus,
   O the word of Jesus,
   it cleanses white as snow!

3 O the love of Jesus,
   O the love of Jesus,
   O the love of Jesus,
   it makes my body whole!

99 Pat Uhl Howard

O what a gift! What a wonderful gift! –
who can tell the wonders of the Lord?
Let us open our eyes and our ears and our hearts –
it is Christ the Lord, it is he!

1 In the stillness of the night
   when the world was asleep,
   the almighty word leapt out;
   he came to Mary, he came to us –
   Christ came to the land of Galilee.
   Christ our Lord and our king!
      O what a gift . . . !

JESUS PRAISE

2 On the night before he died
  it was Passover night,
  and he gathered his friends together.
  He broke the bread, he blessed the wine;
  it was the gift of his love and his life.
  Christ our Lord and our king!
    O what a gift...!

3 On the hill of Calvary
  while the world held its breath,
  it was there for us all to see;
  God gave his Son, his only Son,
  for the love of you and me –
  Christ our Lord and our king!
    O what a gift...!

4 It was early on that morning
  when the guards were asleep,
  back to life came he!
  He conquered death, he conquered sin –
  but victory he gave to you and me,
  Christ our Lord and our king!
    O what a gift...!

5 Some day with the saints
  we will come before our Father,
  and then we will shout and dance and sing!
  For in our midst for our eyes to see
  will be Christ our Lord and our king,
  Christ our Lord and our king!
    O what a gift...!

THE LORD JESUS CHRIST

100

A. W. Edsor

On Calvary's tree he died for me,
that I his love might know;
to set me free he died for me –
that's why I love him so.

101

Roy Tanner

Precious Jesus, precious Jesus,
you have brought us back from death;
through your love you made us new, Lord,
and we thank you most of all!
You are king, Lord;
prince of peace, Lord;
living saviour, great redeemer:
O how we love you,
O how we love you!

from Song of Solomon 2
Hugh Pollock

1 See him like a gazelle
   leaping over the mountains,
   bounding over the hills:
   my beloved One comes!

   Turtledoves sing in the land
   bringing the season of glad song;
   my beloved is mine,
   and he tells me to come.

2 Hear him lifting his voice –
   such a sweet invitation,
   see him stand by my side:
   my beloved One comes!
   Turtledoves sing...

3 First figs seen on the tree –
   blossom of vine gives its fragrance,
   vineyards bursting in flower:
   my beloved One comes!
   Turtledoves sing...

4 See, the winter is past,
   rain is over and gone now,
   flowers appear on the earth:
   my beloved One comes!
   Turtledoves sing...

THE LORD JESUS CHRIST

103 Michael Perry

1 See him lying on a bed of straw;
  a draughty stable with an open door;
  Mary cradling the babe she bore –
  the prince of glory is his name:

  O now carry me to Bethlehem
  to see the Lord appear to men;
  just as poor as was the stable then,
  the prince of glory when he came.

2 Star of silver sweep across the skies,
  show where Jesus in the manger lies;
  shepherds swiftly from your stupor rise
  to see the saviour of the world:
  O now carry . . .

3 Angels, sing again the song you sang,
  bring God's glory to the heart of man;
  sing that Bethl'em's little baby can
  be salvation to the soul:
  O now carry . . .

4 Mine are riches – from your poverty,
  from your innocence, eternity;
  mine, forgiveness by your death for me,
  child of sorrow for my joy:
  O now carry . . .

104

1 Sing alleluia to the Lord,
  sing alleluia to the Lord;
    sing alleluia, sing alleluia,
  sing alleluia to the Lord!

2 Jesus is risen from the dead,
  Jesus is risen from the dead;
    Jesus is risen, Jesus is risen,
  Jesus is risen from the dead.

3 Jesus is Lord of heaven and earth,
  Jesus is Lord of heaven and earth;
    Jesus is Lord, Jesus is Lord,
  Jesus is Lord of heaven and earth.

4 Jesus is living in his church,
  Jesus is living in his church;
    Jesus is living, Jesus is living,
  Jesus is living in his church.

5 Jesus is coming for his own,
  Jesus is coming for his own;
    Jesus is coming, Jesus is coming,
  Jesus is coming for his own.

THE LORD JESUS CHRIST

Somebody's knocking at your door,
somebody's knocking at your door;
O sinner why don't you answer?
somebody's knocking at your door.

1 Knocks like Jesus! –
   somebody's knocking at your door.
   Knocks like Jesus! –
   somebody's knocking at your door;
   O sinner why don't you answer?
   somebody's knocking at your door:
      Somebody's knocking...

2 Can't you hear him? –
   somebody's knocking at your door.
   Can't you hear him? –
   somebody's knocking at your door;
   O sinner why don't you answer?
   somebody's knocking at your door:
      Somebody's knocking...

3 Answer Jesus! –
   somebody's knocking at your door.
   Answer Jesus! –
   somebody's knocking at your door;
   O sinner why don't you answer?
   somebody's knocking at your door.

106 Unknown

Sovereign Lord, sovereign Lord,
you made all things by your word;
my creator, redeemer, my King of kings adored,
sovereign Lord, sovereign Lord!

107 after Colossians 2
Unknown

1 The fullness of the Godhead
   bodily dwells in my Lord;
the fullness of the Godhead
   bodily dwells in my Lord;
the fullness of the Godhead
   bodily dwells in my Lord,
and we are complete in him:
   Complete, complete, complete in him,
   we are complete in him.
   Alleluia we're complete,
   complete, complete in him,
   we are complete in him.

2 It's not by works of righteousness
   but by his grace alone;
it's not by works of righteousness
   but by his grace alone;
it's not by works of righteousness
   but by his grace alone
that we are complete in him:
   Complete, complete...

THE LORD JESUS CHRIST

3 There's nothing more that I can do –
     for Jesus did it all;
  there's nothing more that I can do –
     for Jesus did it all;
  there's nothing more that I can do –
     for Jesus did it all,
  and we are complete in him:
     Complete, complete...

108 from John 4
         Unknown

The well is deep and I require
a drink of the water of life;
but none can quench my soul's desire
for a drink of the water of life,
till one draws near who the cry will heed,
helper of men in their time of need;
and I, believing, find indeed
that Christ is the water of life.

109
after Philippians 2, Romans 10
Michael Baughen

1 There's no greater name than Jesus,
   name of him who came to save us;
   in that saving name so gracious
   every knee shall bow:

2 Let everything that is 'neath the ground,
   let everything in the world around,
   let everything that's high o'er the sky
   bow at Jesus' name!

3 In our minds, by faith professing,
   in our hearts, by inward blessing,
   on our tongues, by words confessing
   Jesus Christ is Lord.

110
after 1 Thessalonians 4
Timothy Dudley-Smith

1 We shall see the Lord in glory when he comes,
   we shall see the Lord in glory when he comes;
   as I read the gospel story
   we shall see the Lord in glory,
   we shall see the Lord in glory when he comes!
      With the alleluias ringing to the sky,
      with the alleluias ringing to the sky;
      as I read the gospel story
      we shall see the Lord in glory,
      with the alleluias ringing to the sky!

THE LORD JESUS CHRIST

2 We shall hear the trumpet sounded when he comes,
   we shall hear the trumpet sounded when he comes;
   we shall hear the trumpet sounded,
   see the Lord by saints surrounded,
   we shall hear the trumpet sounded when he comes!
      With the alleluias ringing to the sky,
      with the alleluias ringing to the sky;
      we shall hear the trumpet sounded,
      see the Lord by saints surrounded,
      with the alleluias ringing to the sky!

3 We shall all rise up to meet him when he comes,
   we shall all rise up to meet him when he comes,
   when he calls his own to greet him,
   we shall all rise up to meet him,
   we shall all rise up to meet him when he comes!
      With the alleluias ringing to the sky,
      with the alleluias ringing to the sky;
      when he calls his own to meet him,
      we shall all rise up to meet him,
      with the alleluias ringing to the sky!

Version 1

1 What a wonderful saviour is Jesus!
   what a wonderful friend is he;
   for he left all the glory of heaven,
   came to earth to die on Calvary:

     Sing hosanna, sing hosanna
     sing hosanna to the King of kings!
     Sing hosanna, sing hosanna,
     sing hosanna to the King!

2 He arose from the grave –alleluia!
   and he lives never more to die;
   at the Father's right hand interceding,
   he will hear and heed our faintest cry:
     Sing hosanna . . . !

3 He is coming some day to receive us –
   we'll be caught up to heaven above;
   what a joy it will be to behold him –
   sing forever of his grace and love!
     Sing hosanna . . . !

Version 2

1 Give me joy in my heart, keep me praising!
   give me joy in my heart, I pray;
   Give me joy in my heart, keep me praising,
   keep me praising till the break of day:

THE LORD JESUS CHRIST

Sing hosanna, sing hosanna
sing hosanna to the King of kings!
Sing hosanna, sing hosanna,
sing hosanna to the King!

2 Give me peace in my heart, keep me trusting...
  Sing hosanna...!

3 Give me love in my heart, keep me serving...
  Sing hosanna...!

112 Unknown

1 What *grace! – God gave us his Son,
  what *grace, God gave us his Son,
  what *grace, God gave us his Son,
  what *grace, what grace, God gave us his Son;
  what *grace, what grace, God gave us his Son!

2 What *grace! –he died on the Cross...

3 What *grace! – he rose from the grave...

4 What *grace! – he's coming again...

5 What *grace! – alleluia!...

  *Or 'love'...

113   Isaac Watts

1 When I survey the wondrous cross
   on which the prince of glory died,
   my richest gain I count but loss,
   and pour contempt on all my pride.

2 Forbid it, Lord, that I should boast
   save in the cross of Christ my God;
   the very things that charm me most –
   I sacrifice them to his blood.

3 See from his head, his hands, his feet,
   sorrow and love flow mingled down;
   when did such love and sorrow meet,
   or thorns compose so rich a crown?

4 Were the whole realm of nature mine,
   that were an offering far too small;
   love so amazing, so divine,
   demands my soul, my life, my all.

114

Robert Stoodley

1 Who does Jesus love,
   Jesus love, Jesus love?
Who does Jesus love?
   He loves everyone!
Well, everybody should love Jesus,
   should love Jesus,
everybody should love Jesus too!

2 Who does Jesus care for,
   Jesus care for, Jesus care for?
Who does Jesus care for?
   He cares for everyone!
Well, everybody should care for Jesus,
   should care for Jesus,
everybody should care for Jesus, too!

3 Who did Jesus come to serve,
   come to serve, come to serve?
Who did Jesus come to serve?
   He came to serve everyone!
Well, everybody should serve Jesus,
   should serve Jesus,
everybody should serve Jesus, too!

4 What did Jesus say,
   Jesus say, Jesus say?
What did Jesus say?
   He said love everyone!
Well, everybody should love each other,
   should love each other,
everybody should love each other, too!

JESUS PRAISE

5 Who did Jesus die for,
    Jesus die for, Jesus die for?
Who did Jesus die for?
    He died for everyone!
Well, everybody should live for Jesus,
    should live for Jesus,
everybody should live for Jesus, too!

115   Norman Warren

Who is Jesus? Who is Jesus? Who is Jesus? –
would you like to know?

1 He's God's Son from heaven, that's who Jesus is;
  Who is Jesus? Who is Jesus? Who is Jesus? –
  would you like to know?

2 He's our Lord and saviour...
  Who is Jesus...?

3 He's the king of glory...
  Who is Jesus...?

4 He's our loving shepherd...
  Who is Jesus...?

5 He's the judge of all men...
  Who is Jesus...?

116
from Malachi 4
Unknown

1 With healing in his wings,
with healing in his wings,
the sun of righteousness shall rise,
with healing in his wings.

2 Lord Jesus now heal me,
Lord Jesus, now heal me!
The sun of righteousness shall rise –
Lord Jesus, now heal me!

117
Norman Warren

1 With my heart I worship you –
Jesus, Jesus;
with my heart I worship you –
Jesus, Jesus:
you gave all in love for me,
saved me for eternity;
with my heart I worship you!

2 With my lips I praise you...

3 With my life I serve you...

118 Norman Warren

Without me you can do nothing,
without me there is no loving,
without me there is no growing,
without me there is no knowing
    the Father's gift of love; (life/joy/peace)
    the Father's gift of love. (life/joy/peace)

119 after Psalm 19, 119; Proverbs 24 etc.
Unknown

1 Wonderful and marvellous is Jesus to me,
  sweeter than the honey in the honey-comb is he:
  Jesus is real, he'll never fail,
  I will serve him now and throughout all eternity.

2 He is always with me as I'm walking along
  I can hear a melody – he's given me a song:
  Jesus is real, he'll never fail,
  I will serve him now and throughout all eternity.

120
after Isaiah 9, Malachi 4, Hebrews 1, John 6, Matthew 21 *etc.*
Mavis Ford

You are the king of glory, you are the prince of peace,
you are the Lord of heaven and earth,
you're the sun of righteousness!
Angels bow down before you, worship and adore,
for you have the words of eternal life,
you are Jesus Christ the Lord!
  Hosanna to the Son of David,
  hosanna to the King of Kings!
  Glory in the highest heaven
  for Jesus the messiah reigns!

121
from Revelation 4 and 5
Pauline Michael Mills and Tom Smail

1 You are worthy, you are worthy,
   you are worthy, O Lord;
   you are worthy to receive glory,
   glory and honour and power:
   for you have created, have all things created,
   for you have created all things;
   and for your pleasure they are created;
   you are worthy, O Lord!

JESUS PRAISE

2 You are worthy, you are worthy,
   you are worthy, O Lamb;
   you are worthy to receive glory,
   and power at the Father's right hand:
   for you have redeemed us,
       have ransomed and cleaned us
   by your blood making us new;
   in white robes arrayed us,
       kings and priests made us,
   and we are reigning in you.

THE HOLY SPIRIT

122 Unknown

1 All over the world the Spirit is moving,
  all over the world as the prophet said it would be;
  all over the world there's a mighty revelation
  of the glory of the Lord, as the waters cover the sea.

2 Deep down in my heart the Spirit is moving,
  deep down in my heart as the prophet said it would be;
  deep down in my heart there's a mighty revelation
  of the glory of the Lord, as the waters cover the sea.

123 W. J. Graham Hobson

1 Kept by the power of God,
  kept by the power of God;
    day by day,
    come what may,
  kept by the power of God.

2 Kept by the love of God,
  kept by the love of God;
    day by day,
    come what may,
  kept by the love of God.

3 Kept by the grace of God,
   kept by the grace of God;
      day by day,
      come what may,
   kept by the grace of God.

4 Kept by the Spirit of God,
   kept by the Spirit of God;
      day by day,
      come what may,
   kept by the Spirit of God.

124 Graham Kendrick

1 Let me have my way among you,
   do not strive, do not strive.   *Repeat*
   For mine is the power and the glory
   for ever and ever the same.
   Let me have my way among you,
   do not strive, do not strive.

2 We'll let you have your way among us,
   we'll not strive, we'll not strive.   *Repea*
   For yours is the power and the glory
   for ever and ever the same.
   We'll let you have your way among us,
   we'll not strive, we'll not strive.

3 Let my peace rule within your hearts,
  do not strive, do not strive. *Repeat*
  For mine is the power and the glory
  for ever and ever the same.
  Let my peace rule within your hearts,
  do not strive, do not strive.

4 We'll let your peace rule within our hearts
  we'll not strive, we'll not strive. *Repeat*
  For yours...*etc.*

125

Norman Warren

1 O Holy Spirit breathe on me,
  O Holy Spirit breathe on me
  and cleanse away my sin,
  fill me with love within:
  O Holy Spirit breathe on me!

2 O Holy Spirit fill my life,
  O Holy Spirit fill my life,
  take all my pride from me,
  give me humility:
  O Holy Spirit breathe on me!

3 O Holy Spirit make me new,
   O Holy Spirit make me new,
   make Jesus real to me,
   give me his purity:
   O Holy Spirit breathe on me!

4 O Holy Spirit wind of God,
   O Holy Spirit wind of God,
   give me your power today,
   to live for you always:
   O Holy Spirit breathe on me!

126 Traditional

Ruach, Ruach, Ruach, Ruach,
Ruach, Ruach, Ruach, Ruach:
   Not by might or power
   but by the Spirit of God;
   not by might or power
   but by the Spirit of God:
Ruach, Ruach, Ruach, Ruach,
Ruach, Ruach, Ruach, Ruach!

Ruach is the Hebrew word for 'spirit', 'wind', or 'breath'.

127   Margaret Old

Spirit of God, unseen as the wind,
gentle as is the dove:
teach us the truth and help us believe,
show us the saviour's love!

1 You spoke to men long, long ago,
   gave us the written word;
   we read it still, needing its truth
   through it God's voice is heard.
       Spirit of God...!

2 Without your help we fail our Lord,
   we cannot live his way;
   we need your power, we need your strength,
   following Christ each day.
       Spirit of God...!

128   Daniel Iverson
          verse 2: Michael Baughen

1 Spirit of the living God, fall afresh on me,
   Spirit of the living God, fall afresh on me:
   break me, melt me, mould me, fill me –
   Spirit of the living God, fall afresh on me!

2 Spirit of the living God, move among us all,
   make us one in heart and mind, make us one in love:
   humble, caring, selfless, sharing –
   Spirit of the living God, fill our lives with love!

THE HOLY SPIRIT

129 Unknown

Thank you, God, for sending Jesus;
thank you, Jesus, that you came;
Holy Spirit, won't you tell us
    more about his wondrous name?

130 Graham Kendrick

1 Where the Spirit of the Lord is,
  where the Spirit of the Lord is,
  there is liberty, there is liberty;
  where the Spirit of the Lord is,
  where the Spirit of the Lord is,
  there is liberty, there is liberty:
    And I will praise you O Lord,
    and I will praise you O Lord,
    and I will praise you O Lord
    in the Spirit;
    and I will praise...

2 Where the power of the Lord is,
  where the power of the Lord is,
  there is victory, there is victory;
  where the power of the Lord is,
  where the power of the Lord is,
  there is victory, there is victory:
    And I will triumph, O Lord,
    and I will triumph, O Lord,
    and I will triumph, O Lord,
    in the Spirit;
    and I will triumph...

3 Where the presence of the Lord is,
   where the presence of the Lord is,
   there is fullness of joy, there is fullness of joy;
   where the presence of the Lord is,
   where the presence of the Lord is,
   there is fullness of joy, there is fullness of joy:
       And I will enjoy you, O Lord,
       and I will enjoy you, O Lord,
       and I will enjoy you, O Lord,
       in the Spirit!
       and I will enjoy...

131   Jane & Betsy Clowe

> *Wind, Wind blow on me;*
> *Wind, Wind set me free!*
> *Wind, Wind – my Father*
> *sent the blessed Holy Spirit:*

1 Jesus told us all about you,
   how we could not live without you,
   with his blood the power bought to
   help us live the life he taught.
       Wind, Wind...

2 When we're weary you console us,
   when we're lonely you enfold us,
   when in danger you uphold us,
   blessed holy Spirit.
       Wind, Wind...

3 When into the church you came,
   it was not in your own but Jesus' name:
   Jesus Christ is still the same –
   he sends the Holy Spirit.
   Wind, Wind...

4 Set us free to love our brothers,
   set us free to live for others,
   that the world the Son might see
   and Jesus' name exalted be.
   Wind, Wind...

FELLOWSHIP
AND THE CHURCH

132 from John 13
Unknown

A new commandment that I give to you,
  is to love one another as I have loved you;
  is to love one another as I have loved you.
By this shall all men know you are my disciples:
  if you have love one for another;
by this shall all men know you are my disciples:
  if you have love one for another.

133 from Ephesians 4
B. Gillman

Bind us together Lord,
bind us together
with cords that cannot be broken;
bind us together Lord,
bind us together,
O bind us together in love!

1 There is only one God,
  there is only one King,
  there is only one Body –
  that is why we sing:
    Bind us together...

2 Made for the glory of God,
  purchased by his precious Son,
  born with the right to be clean,
  for Jesus the victory has won:
    Bind us together...

3 You are the family of God,
   you are the promise divine,
   you are God's chosen desire,
   you are the glorious new wine:
       Bind us together . . .

134   Colin and Janet Lunt

Broken for me, broken for you,
the body of Jesus broken for you;
broken for me, broken for you
the body of Jesus broken for you.

1 He offered his body, he poured out his soul,
   Jesus was broken that we might be whole:
       Broken for me . . .

2 Come to my table and with me dine,
   eat of my bread and drink of my wine:
       Broken for me . . .

3 This is my body given for you,
   eat it remembering I died for you:
       Broken for me . . .

4 This is my blood I shed for you,
   for your forgiveness, making you new:
       Broken for me . . .

135

from Psalm 87
Lenny Smith

1 City, O city, O city of God,
glorious things are spoken of you;
city, O city, O city of God,
glorious things are spoken of you:
Such glorious things are spoken of you,
city, O city, O city of God;
glorious things are spoken of you!

2 This one and that one were born in her –
all my springs of joy are in you;
this one and that one were born in her –
all my springs of joy are in you:
Yes all my springs of joy are in you,
this one and that one were born in her;
all my springs of joy are in you!

3 Singers and dancers together say,
all my springs of joy are in you;
singers and dancers together say,
all my springs of joy are in you:
Yes all my springs of joy are in you,
singers and dancers together say,
all my springs of joy are in you!

136 after Luke 2
Unknown

1 Come and go with me to my Father's house,
to my Father's house, to my Father's house;
come and go with me to my Father's house
where there's joy, joy, joy!

2 It's not very far to my Father's house,
to my Father's house, to my Father's house;
come and go with me to my Father's house
where there's joy, joy, joy!

3 There is room for all in my Father's house,
in my Father's house, in my Father's house;
come and go with me to my Father's house
where there's joy, joy, joy!

4 Everything is free in my father's house,
in my Father's house, in my Father's house;
come and go with me to my Father's house
where there's joy, joy, joy!

5 Jesus is the way to my Father's house,
to my Father's house, to my Father's house;
come and go with me to my Father's house
where there's joy, joy, joy!

6 Jesus is the light in my father's house,
in my Father's house, in my Father's house;
come and go with me to my Father's house
where there's joy, joy, joy!

JESUS PRAISE

137 from 2 Corinthians 13

1 The grace of our Lord Jesus Christ,
  the love of God,
  the fellowship of the Holy Spirit
    be with us all, evermore.

2 The grace of our Lord Jesus Christ,
  the love of God,
  the fellowship of the Holy Spirit
    be with us all, evermore,
    evermore. Amen.

This may be sung with the people repeating
each phrase after a soloist.

138 from 2 Corinthians 13
Steve Raven

The grace of our Lord Jesus Christ,
the love of God,
the fellowship of the Holy Spirit
be with us all.

1 We are people in *(   ),
  we want you to work in our land:
  so take us and mould us,
  and lead us but hold us,
  and teach us to understand!
    The grace...

*Britain, America

2 You give us our love for each other
that you might be seen where we live:
so help us to show it
as others might know it –
we need you to help us to give.

The grace of our Lord Jesus Christ,
the love of God,
the fellowship of the Holy Spirit
be with us all for evermore. Amen.

139   Jimmy Owens

1 He is here, he is here,
he is moving among us;
he is here, he is here
as we gather in his name!
He is here, he is here,
and he wants to work a wonder;
he is here as we gather in his name.

2 He is Lord, he is Lord,
let us worship before him;
he is Lord, he is Lord,
as we gather in his name!
He is Lord, he is Lord,
let us praise and adore him –
yesterday and today
and for evermore the same.

140 Steve Stone

1 He is here (Jesus is here),
   he is here (Jesus is here):
   *my heart tells me
      he is here (Jesus, Jesus is here).

2 He is Lord (Jesus is Lord!),
   he is Lord (Jesus is Lord!):
   *my heart tells me
      he is Lord (Jesus, Jesus is Lord).

3 I will praise him (Jesus is Lord!),
   I will praise him (Jesus is Lord!):
   *my heart tells me
      he is Lord (Jesus, Jesus is Lord).

* Or 'God's word tells me ...'

141 Graham Kendrick

1 Jesus stand among us at the meeting of our lives,
   be our sweet agreement at the meeting of our eyes:
   O Jesus we love you, so we gather here –
   join our hearts in unity, and take away our fear.

2 So to you we're gathering out of each and every land,
   Christ the love between us at the joining of our hands:
   O Jesus we love you, so we gather here –
   join our hearts in unity, and take away our fear.

FELLOWSHIP AND THE CHURCH

3 Jesus stand among us at the meeting of our lives,
   be our sweet agreement at the meeting of our eyes:
   O Jesus we love you, so we gather here –
   join our hearts in unity, and take away our fear.

142 Version 1
        Unknown

1 Let us break bread together on our knees,
   let us break bread together on our knees:
      When I fall on my knees,
      with my face to the rising sun,
      O Lord, have mercy on me!

2 Let us drink wine together on our knees,
   let us drink wine together on our knees:
      When I fall . . .

3 Let us praise God together on our knees,
   let us praise God together on our knees:
      When I fall . . .

Version 2
Jim Seddon

1 Let us praise God together,
      let us praise;
   Let us praise God together
      all our days:
   he is faithful in all his ways,
   he is worthy of all our praise,
   his name be exalted on high!

JESUS PRAISE

2 Let us seek God together,
       let us pray;
   let us seek his forgiveness
       as we pray:
   he will cleanse us from all sin,
   he will help us the fight to win,
   his name be exalted on high!

3 Let us serve God together,
       him obey;
   let our lives show his goodness
       through each day:
   Christ the Lord is the world's true light –
   let us serve him with all our might,
   his name be exalted on high!

143   from Acts 3
          Unknown

Peter and John went to pray,
they met a lame man on the way;
he asked for alms, and held out his palms,
and this is what Peter did say:

Silver and gold have I none,
but such as I have I give you:
in the name of Jesus Christ of Nazareth
rise up and walk!

He went walking and leaping and praising God,
walking and leaping and praising God.
'In the name of Jesus Christ of Nazareth,
rise up and walk!'

FELLOWSHIP AND THE CHURCH

144

Tedd Smith

1 There's a quiet understanding
    when we gather in the Spirit;
  it's a promise that he gives us
    when we gather in his name:

2 There's a love we feel in Jesus –
    living bread he longs to feed us;
  it's a promise that he gives us
    when we gather in his name:

3 And we know when we're together,
    sharing love and understanding,
  that our brothers and our sisters
    feel the oneness that he brings:

4 Thank you Jesus, thank you Jesus,
    for the way you love and feed us;
  for the many ways you lead us,
    thank you Lord, thank you Lord!

145 Charles High

This is the day of the Lord,
this is the day of the Lord,
this is the day of the Lord,
Alleluia, alleluia!

Other verses:

This is the (feast...birthday...service...song)
  of the Lord...

We are the people of the Lord...

These are the praises of the Lord...

146 from Psalm 118 Unknown

1 This is the day, this is the day,
   that the Lord has made, that the Lord has made;
   we will rejoice, we will rejoice,
   and be glad in it, and be glad in it:
      This is the day that the Lord has made,
      we will rejoice and be glad in it;
      this is the day, this is the day,
      that the Lord has made.

2 This is the day when he rose again...

3 This is the day when the Spirit came...

FELLOWSHIP AND THE CHURCH

147 after Numbers 6
Michael Perry

1 To God's loving-kindness we commit you,
   the Lord bless your life and make you strong.
      May the praises of God,
      the Father and the Son
      and the Spirit – Three-in-One,
   be your song.

2 To God's holy favour we commend you,
   the Lord hear your prayers and show his face.
      And the mercy of God,
      the Father and the Son
      and the Spirit – Three-in-One,
   bring you grace.

3 To God's great protection we entrust you,
   the Lord take your hand and give you peace.
      Let the blessing of God,
      the Father and the Son
      and the Spirit – Three-in-One,
   never cease.

148 from Ephesians 4 and 1 Corinthians 12
Michael Perry

1 We are one body in the Lord,
we have one Spirit and one call;
there is
   one hope,
   one Lord,
   one faith,
   one life,
one Father of us all!

2 There are some who can tend the flock,
there are some who can preach the word,
so that
   some lead,
   some serve,
   some teach,
   some build
one body in the Lord.

149

Bruce Ballinger

1 We have come into his house,
   and gathered in his name to worship him;
we have come into his house,
   and gathered in his name to worship him;
we have come into his house,
   and gathered in his name
   to worship Christ the Lord,
worship him, Christ the Lord.

2 Let's forget about ourselves
   and concentrate on him and worship him;
let's forget about ourselves
   and concentrate on him and worship him;
let's forget about ourselves
   and concentrate on him
   and worship Christ the Lord,
worship him, Christ the Lord.

3 He is all our righteousness,
   we stand complete in him and worship him;
he is all our righteousness,
   we stand complete in him and worship him;
he is all our righteousness,
   we stand complete in him
   and worship Christ the Lord,
worship him, Christ the Lord.

150

from Revelation 3, 4 etc.
Norman Warren

*We will come into his presence
with thanksgiving in our hearts,
we will come into his presence
with thanksgiving in our hearts,
singing:*

1 Holy, holy is the Lord,
   holy, holy is the Lord!
   We will come...

2 Worthy is the Lamb that died
   worthy is the Lamb that died!
   We will come...

3 Glory to our risen king,
   glory to our risen king!
   We will come...

4 Jesus Christ is Lord of all,
   Jesus Christ is Lord of all!
   We will come...

5 Holy, holy is the Lord,
   holy, holy is the Lord!
   We will come...

FELLOWSHIP AND THE CHURCH

PRAYER
AND THE BIBLE

151

Unknown

1 All my heart I give to you, O Lord;
   all my heart I give to you:
   I give to you as you gave to me –
   all my heart I give to you.

2 You suffered for the sake of man
   that we might live in you:
   O may we show our thankfulness
   in all we say and do!

3 All my life I give to you, O Lord;
   all my life I give to you:
   I give to you as you gave to me –
   all my life I give to you.

4 Sing glory to the Father,
   sing glory to the Son,
   sing glory to the Spirit –
   to God the Three-in-One.

5 All myself I give to you, O Lord;
   all myself I give to you:
   I give to you as you gave to me –
   all myself I give to you.

152 from 2 Timothy 3
Michael Baughen

1 All Scriptures are given by the breath of God
  are inspired of God,
  are the word of the Lord;
  all Scriptures are given by the breath of God,
  and glorify his name!
    They can make you wise to a saving faith
    in Jesus Christ the Lord;
    they can make the man of God complete,
    and are meant to be his sword!

2 So study to show yourself approved to God,
  fit to use his word,
  fit to speak in his name;
  so study to show yourself approved to God,
  a workman not ashamed:
    They'll reprove, correct, and a training in
    all righteous living afford;
    they will yield up all that we need to know
    of the teaching of the Lord!

3 All Scriptures are given by the breath of God,
  are inspired of God,
  are the word of the Lord;
  all Scriptures are given by the breath of God,
  and glorify his name!

153 from Psalm 46
Unknown

1 Be still and know that I am God,
   be still and know that I am God,
   be still and know that I am God!

2 I am the Lord who heals your pain...

3 In you, O Lord, I put my trust...

154 M. A. Lathbury

Break now the bread of life,
   dear Lord, to me,
as you once broke the loaves beside the sea:
beyond the sacred page I seek you Lord –
my spirit longs for you, O Living Word!

PRAYER AND THE BIBLE

155

1 Come Lord Jesus, come Lord Jesus,
   come and make our hearts your home! –
   we bow before you, we love and adore you,
   acknowledge that you are Lord of all:
   Come Lord Jesus, come Lord Jesus,
   come and make our hearts your home.

2 Come Lord Jesus, come Lord Jesus,
   come and make our hearts your throne! –
   we bow before you, we love and adore you,
   acknowledge that you are Lord of all:
   Come Lord Jesus, come Lord Jesus,
   come and make our hearts your throne.

3 Come Lord Jesus, come Lord Jesus,
   come and make this world your own! –
   we bow before you, we love and adore you,
   acknowledge that you are Lord of all:
   Come Lord Jesus, come Lord Jesus,
   come and make this world your own.

156 after Richard of Chichester

Day by day, day by day,
dear Lord, of you three things I pray:
   to see you more clearly,
   to love you more dearly,
   to follow you more nearly,
day by day;
   to see you more clearly,
   to love you more dearly,
   to follow you more nearly
day by day, day by day!

157 Unknown

1 Dona nobis pacem, pacem;
  dona nobis pacem!
  Dona nobis pacem;
  dona nobis pacem!
  Dona nobis pacem;
  dona nobis pacem!

2 Give us, give us, give us your peace;
  give, give us, give us your peace!
  Give us, give us your peace:
  give us, give us, give us your peace!
  Give us, give us your peace;
  give us, give us, give us your peace!

Sing as a round

158 Traditional

1 Kum ba yah, my Lord, kum ba yah,
   kum ba yah, my Lord, kum ba yah,
   kum ba yah, my Lord, kum ba yah:
   O Lord, kum ba yah!

2 Someone's crying Lord, kum ba yah...!

3 Someone's singing Lord, kum ba yah...!

4 Someone's praying Lord, kum ba yah...!

Kum ba yah – 'Come by here'

159 from the 'Evening Collect'
Chris Humphries

Lighten our darkness, Lord, we pray;
and in your mercy, and in your mercy defend us
from all perils and dangers of this night:
lighten our darkness for the love of your only Son,
our saviour Jesus Christ.   Amen.

160

Traditional

1 Lord, I want to be a Christian
   in my heart, in my heart;
Lord, I want to be a Christian
   in my heart, in my heart, in my heart;
Lord, I want to be a Christian in my heart!

2 Lord, I want to be more loving
   in my heart . . .

3 Lord, I want to be more holy
   in my heart . . .

4 Lord, I want to be like Jesus
   in my heart . . .

161

after a prayer attributed to St. Francis of Assisi

1 Make me a channel of your peace:
where there is hatred let me bring your love,
where there is injury, your pardon Lord
and where there's doubt, true faith in you:
   O Master grant that I may never seek
   so much to be consoled as to console;
   to be understood as to understand,
   to be loved, as to love with all my soul!

2 Make me a channel of your peace:
   where there's despair in life let me bring hope,
   where there is darkness, only light,
   and where there's sadness, ever joy:
      O Master grant that I may never seek
      so much to be consoled as to console;
      to be understood as to understand,
      to be loved, as to love with all my soul!

3 Make me a channel of your peace:
   it is in pardoning that we are pardoned,
   in giving of ourselves that we receive,
   and in dying that we're born to eternal life.
      O Master grant that I may never seek
      so much to be consoled as to console;
      to be understood as to understand,
      to be loved, as to love with all my soul!

   Repeat verse 1 without chorus

162   after Mother Theresa of Calcutta

   1 Make us worthy, Lord,
      to serve our fellow men
      throughout the world
      who live in poverty and hunger,
      in poverty and hunger,
      in poverty and hunger.

2 Give them through our hands,
   this day their daily bread,
   and by our understanding love,
   give peace and joy,
   give peace and joy,
   give peace and joy.

163   2 Corinthians 13
          St. Aidan's Community

May the grace of our Lord Jesus Christ
and the love of God our Father,
and the fellowship, the fellowship
   of the Holy Spirit
be with us for evermore
and evermore, and evermore.   Amen.

164   from John 12
          Robert Cull

Open our eyes, Lord,
   we want to see Jesus –
to reach out and touch him
and say that we love him;
open our ears, Lord,
   and help us to listen:
O open our eyes, Lord,
   we want to see Jesus!

165

from 'The Lord's Prayer', Matthew 6 and Luke 11
David Peacock

1 *Soloist:* Our Father in heaven,
People: Our Father in heaven,

S: holy is your name:
P: holy is your name:

S: may your kingdom come, O Lord;
P: may your kingdom come, O Lord;

S: may your will be done here on earth
P: may your will be done here on earth

S: as it is in heaven.
P: as it is in heaven.

S: Give us the food we need for today.
P: Give us the food we need for today.

S: Please forgive us the sins we have done,
P: Please forgive us the sins we have done,

S: as we forgive
P: as we forgive

S: the sins that others have done to us
P: the sins that others have done to us

S:	Do not bring us to hard testing,
P:	Do not bring us to hard testing,

S:	and protect us from all evil, Lord!
P:	and protect us from all evil, Lord!

2   For yours is the kingdom
and the power and glory;
yours is the kingdom,
the power, and the glory,
for ever and ever,
Amen. Amen. Amen.

for ever, Lord,
Amen. Amen. Amen.

166   <small>H. H. Lemmel</small>

Turn your eyes upon Jesus,
look full in his wonderful face;
and the things of earth will grow strangely dim
in the light of his glory and grace!

167

from Psalm 25
Unknown

1 Unto you O Lord, (unto you O Lord,)
  do I lift up my soul, (do I lift up my soul;)
  unto you O Lord, (unto you O Lord,)
  do I lift up my soul, (do I lift up my soul:)

  O my God, (O my God,)
  I trust in you, (I trust in you _)
  let me not be ashamed,
  let not my enemies triumph over me!

2 Show me your ways, (show me your ways,)
  your ways O Lord, (your ways O Lord;)
  teach me your paths, (teach me your paths,)
  your paths O Lord, (your paths O Lord:)
      O my God...

3 Remember not, (remember not)
  the sins of my youth, (the sins of my youth;)
  remember not, (remember not,)
  the sins of my youth, (the sins of my youth:)
      O my God...

4 The secret of the Lord, (the secret of the Lord)
  is with them that love him, (with them that love him:)
  the secret of the Lord, (the secret of the Lord)
  is with them that love him, (is with them that love him;)
      O my God...

168 from Isaiah 26 and John 14
Norman Warren

1 You will keep him in perfect peace,
   you will keep him in perfect peace
   whose mind is stayed on you,
   because he trusts in you:
   trust in the Lord for ever!

2 Let not your heart be troubled,
   neither let it be afraid:
   'My peace I leave with you,
   my peace I give to you;
   not as the world give I to you!'

THE CHRISTIAN LIFE

169 Horace R. Jones

> All that I am he made me,
> all that I have he gave me;
> and all that ever I hope to be,
> Jesus alone must do for me.

170 from Jeremiah 29
Robert Rhodes

And you shall seek me, and you shall find me
when you shall search for me with all your heart;
and I will be found of you, and I will be found of you
when you shall seek me with all your heart.
And I will be found of you, and I will be found of you,
when you shall seek me with all your heart.

171 from Galatians 5
Michael Baughen

> *Bring forth the fruit of the Spirit in your life,*
> *let the life of Christ be seen in you;*
> *bring forth the fruit of the Spirit in your life,*
> *and let the Lord be glorified in you!*

> Seek his patience and his kindness,
> seek his gentleness and self control;
> seek his goodness and his faithfulness,
> and seek most his peace, and joy, and love.
>   *Bring forth..!*

172   from Psalm 137
Michael Perry

1 By flowing waters of Babylon
   we hung our harps on the willows;
   how shall we sing our Jehovah's song
   in a foreign land, far away?

2 They who oppress us and mock our grief
   tell us to sing and be merry;
   how can we worship when spirits fail
   in an alien land far away?

3 If we forget you, Jerusalem,
   may we keep silence for ever! –
   still we remember our distant home
   in another land far away.

173   from Psalm 137

By the waters, the waters of Babylon
we lay down and wept
   and wept for you, Zion:
we remember, we remember
we remember you, Zion.

174 after Philippians 1
Gary Garcia

Christ in me is to live –
  to die is to gain,
Christ in me is to live –
  to die is to gain;
He's my king, he's my song,
  he's my life and he's my joy;
he's my strength, he's my sword,
  he's my peace and he's my Lord!
Christ in me is to live –
  to die is to gain,
Christ in me is to live –
  to die is to gain!

175 R. Hudson Pope

Cleanse me from my sin Lord,
put your power within Lord,
take me as I am Lord,
and make me all your own:
keep me day by day Lord,
underneath your sway Lord;
make my heart your palace
and your royal throne.

176 Unknown

1 Come, go with me to that land,
  come, go with me to that land,
  come go with me to that land
    where I'm bound:
  come, go with me to that land,
  come, go with me to that land,
  to that land, to that land,
    where I'm bound!

2 I'll see Jesus in that land...
    where I'm bound:..

3 All God's people will be there...
    where I'm bound:..

4 There'll be peace in that land...
    where I'm bound:..

177 from John 14
G. Taylor

1 Do not be worried and upset,
  believe in God, believe also in me:
  there are many rooms in my Father's house,
  and I'm going to prepare a place,
  prepare a place for you.

  I am the way, the truth and the life;
  no one goes to the Father except by me.
  I am the way, the truth and the life,
  and I'm going to prepare a place,
  prepare a place for you.

2 After I go and prepare a place for you,
  I will come back and take you to myself,
  so that you may come and be where I am,
  and I'm going to prepare a place,
  prepare a place for you.
  I am the way...

178 from Luke 6 and Matthew 7
C. R. Vaughan

1 Do not judge others, and God will not judge you,
don't condemn others and God won't condemn you,
forgive the others and God will forgive you,
give to others and God will give to you!

Speck, speck, speck
in your brother's eye,
log, log, log
in your own eye, eye, eye, eye, eye:
take the log out
of your own eye, eye,
to see the speck, speck, speck
in your brother's eye!

2 Ask and you will receive, seek and you will find,
knock and the door will be opened from behind,
do for others what you want them to do,
give to others and God will give to you!
Speck, speck, speck...

3 Would you give a stone when your son asks for bread,
or give a snake when he asks for fish instead?
Bad as you are, you know how to give the good –
give to others, and God will give to you!
Speck, speck, speck...

179 from Philippians 1
J. White

1 For me to live is Christ, to die is gain,
   to hold his hand, and walk his narrow way;
   there is no peace, no joy, no thrill,
   like walking in his will –
   for me to live is Christ, to die is gain.

2 Now once my heart was full of sin and shame,
   till someone told me Jesus came to save;
   when he said 'Come home to me!'
   he set my poor heart free –
   for me to live is Christ, to die is gain.

3 Now there are things that I still do not know,
   but of this one thing I'm completely sure:
   he who called me on that day,
   washed all my sin away –
   for me to live is Christ, to die is gain!

4 For me to live is Christ, to die is gain,
   to hold his hand, and walk his narrow way;
   there is no peace, no joy, no thrill,
   like walking in his will –
   for me to live is Christ, to die is gain.

180   from Isaiah 43 and Matthew 3
         C. R. Vaughan

1 From the distant east and the furthest west,
  I will bring my people home:
  let my people return from the distant lands,
  I will bring my people home.

  Someone is shouting in the desert:
  prepare a road for the Lord,
  make a path straight for him to travel,
  prepare a road for the Lord,
  turn away from your sins!

2 Do not cling to the past or the long ago –
  I will bring my people home:
  I will make a road and the river flow,
  I will bring my people home.
    Someone is shouting...

3 Do not be afraid, through the waters deep,
  I will bring my people home;
  do not be afraid as you pass through fire,
  I will bring my people home:
    Someone is shouting...

Turn away from your sins,
turn away from your sins!

181 Unknown

Go, tell it on the mountain,
over the hills and everywhere;
go, tell it on the mountain
that Jesus Christ is Lord!

1 O when I was a seeker
I sought both night and day,
I asked the Lord to help me,
and he showed me the way:
Go, tell it on the mountain...

2 Then he made me a watchman,
upon the city wall,
to tell of his salvation,
for Jesus died for all:
Go, tell it on the mountain...

3 Go tell it to your neighbour
in darkness here below,
go with the words of Jesus,
that all the world may know:
Go, tell it on the mountain...

182 from Matthew 10 and Matthew 28
Carol Owens

1 God forgave my sin in Jesus' name –
I've been born again in Jesus' name,
and in Jesus' name I come to you
to share his love as he told me to:
he said,

> *'Freely, freely you have received _*
> *freely, freely give!*
> *Go in my name, and because you believe,*
> *others will know that I live.'*

2 All power is given in Jesus' name –
in earth and heaven in Jesus' name,
and in Jesus' name I come to you
to share his power as he told me to:
he said,
> *'Freely, freely...'*

183 W. F. Jabusch

> *God has spoken to his people, alleluia!*
> *and his words are words of wisdom, alleluia!*

1 Open your ears, O Christian people,
open your ears and hear the good news;
open your hearts O Royal Priesthood,
God has come to you, God has come to you!
God has spoken...

2 He who has ears to hear his message,
  he who has ears, then let him hear;
  he who would learn the way of wisdom,
  let him hear God's word, let him hear God's word!
      God has spoken...

3 Israel, come to greet the saviour!
  Judah is glad to see his day;
  from east and west the peoples travel,
  he will show the way, he will show the way.
      God has spoken...

184 M. Pendergrass

1 The greatest thing in all my life is knowing you;
  the greatest thing in all my life is knowing you.
      I want to know you more,
      I want to know you more:
  the greatest thing in all my life is knowing you.

2 The greatest thing in all my life is loving you;
  the greatest thing in all my life is loving you.
      I want to love you more,
      I want to love you more:
  the greatest thing in all my life is loving you.

3 The greatest thing in all my life is serving you;
  the greatest thing in all my life is serving you.
      I want to serve you more,
      I want to serve you more:
  the greatest thing in all my life is to serve you more.

THE CHRISTIAN LIFE

185

Ira Stamphill

1 Happiness is to know the saviour,
living a life within his favour,
having a change in my behaviour –
happiness is the Lord.

2 Happiness is a new creation,
'Jesus and me' in close relation,
having a part in his salvation –
happiness is the Lord.

3 Real joy is mine,
no matter if tears may start;
I've found the secret –
Jesus in my heart.

4 Happiness is to be forgiven,
living a life that's worth the living,
taking the road that leads to heaven –
happiness is the Lord,
happiness is the Lord!

186

Don Marsh

1 Help me to know you as I once knew you,
   help me to seek you as I once sought you;
   help me to love you as I once loved you –
   bring me back close, Lord, closer to you:

   Closer to you Lord, closer to you,
   for I have wandered so far from your loving voice;
   I want to love you as I once loved you _
   bring me back close Lord, closer to you!

2 Turn me from sin: now I would be holy,
   in true repentance I humbly come;
   all that I am now and ever will be,
   I gladly surrender into your care:
      Closer to you, Lord . . .

187

from Revelation 19
The Cheam Fellowship

I am covered over with the robe of righteousness
   that Jesus gives to me – gives to me;
I am covered over with the precious blood
   of Jesus, and he lives in me – lives in me:

What a joy it is to know
my heavenly Father loves me so! –
he gives to me my Jesus;
when he looks at me he sees
not what I used to be,
but he sees Jesus.

THE CHRISTIAN LIFE

188 Traditional

1 I am weak but you are strong,
   Jesus, keep me from all wrong;
   I'll be satisfied as long
   as I walk, let me walk close with you:

   Just a closer walk with you
   all of life's long journey through;
   let it be that all I do
   honours you, dear Lord, honours you.

2 In this world of toils and snares,
   if I falter, Lord, who cares;
   who with me my burden shares? –
   none but you, dear Lord, none but you:
   Just a closer walk...

3 When my feeble life is o'er,
   time for me will be no more:
   guide me gently, safely home,
   to your kingdom's shore, to that shore:
   Just a closer walk...

189 Unknown

1 I have decided to follow Jesus,
   I have decided to follow Jesus,
   I have decided to follow Jesus –
   no turning back, no turning back.

2 The cross before me, the world behind me,
   the cross before me, the world behind me,
   the cross before me, the world behind me –
   no turning back, no turning back.

190 Unknown

1 I want to live for Jesus
      every day (every day),
   I want to live for Jesus,
      come what may (come what may):
      Take the world and all its pleasure! –
      I've got a more enduring treasure,
   I want to live for Jesus every day.

2 I'm going to live for Jesus
      every day (every day),
   I'm going to live for Jesus,
      come what may (come what may):
      Take the world and all its pleasure! –
      I've got a more enduring treasure,
   I want to live for Jesus every day.

191 after Matthew 18 etc.
Unknown

1 I was lost but Jesus found me,
   found the sheep that went astray;
   threw his loving arms around me,
   drew me back into his way:
      Alleluia, alleluia,
      alleluia, alleluia!...

2 Glory, glory, alleluia,
   come and bless the Lord our king,
   glory, glory, alleluia,
   with his praise all heaven rings:
      Alleluia! alleluia!
      alleluia! alleluia!...

A two part round

192   from Matthew 16 etc.
Michael Baughen

1 If any man will follow, if any man will follow,
  if any man will follow after my Jesus,
  let him deny himself and let him take up his cross,
  and let him come and follow after my Lord!
      Whosoever will live for self
      will throw his life away –
      Christ gives life to all who follow him.
      What is a man advantaged if he
      gains the whole wide world
      and then loses his soul?

2 If any man will follow, if any man will follow,
  if any man will follow after my Jesus,
  let him deny himself, and let him take up his cross,
  and let him come and follow after my Lord!
      Whosoever will be ashamed of
      Jesus and his words,
      in this sinful age in which we live,
      Jesus the king will be ashamed of
      him in that great day,
      when in glory he comes!

3 If any man will follow, if any man will follow,
  if any man will follow after my Jesus,
  let him deny himself, and let him take up his cross,
  and let him come and follow after my Lord!

  Let him come and follow after my Lord.

193   J. McKenzie
D. Simmons

1 If I tried to live for you Lord, today;
   if I tried to follow your wonderful way,
   then all of my life would be me and not you,
   and none of your glory would ever shine through.

2 Since I first met you, I knew Lord you were the way,
   I tried hard to walk in your footsteps each day,
   but somehow my life didn't glorify you –
   so make me your channel in all that I do.

3 Take each new day, whatever's in store,
   take my whole being and into me pour,
   your power and your Spirit – O make me anew,
   for no one can change me, Lord Jesus, but you.

194   from 2 Chronicles 7
Cyril Squire

1 If my people will be humbled,
   and pray and seek my presence
   and repent of all their evil,
      then from heaven I will hear.

2 If my people will be humbled
   and pray and seek my presence
   and repent of all their evil,
      then will I forgive their sin
      and give healing to their land.

195

Bob Kilpatrick

1 In my life, Lord, be glorified,
    be glorified:
  in my life, Lord, be glorified today!

2 In my song, Lord, be glorified,
    be glorified:
  in my song, Lord, be glorified today!

3 In your church, Lord, be glorified,
    be glorified:
  in your church, Lord, be glorified today!

4 In my speech, Lord, be glorified,
    be glorified:
  in my speech, Lord, be glorified today!

Other verses ad. lib.

196 Graham Kendrick

1 In your way and in your time –
that's how it's going to be in my life;
and in your perfect way
    I'll rest my weary mind,
and as you lead I'll follow close behind:
and in your presence I will know your peace is mine –
in your time there is rest, there is rest.

2 In your way and in your time –
that's how it's going to be in my life;
dear Jesus soothe me now
    till all my strivings cease,
kiss me with the beauty of your peace:
and I will wait and not be anxious at the time –
in your time there is rest, there is rest.

3 In your way and in your time –
that's how it's going to be in my life;
and though some prayers I've prayed
    may seem unanswered yet,
you never come too quickly or too late:
and I will wait and I will not regret the time –
in your time there is rest, there is rest.

197 'Covenant Song', from Jeremiah 31
Christopher Idle

1 The Lord has said that he will be our God
  and we shall be his people:
      for he writes on our hearts
      all the words of his law;
      he forgives all our sin
      and remembers it no more:
  and this is God's new covenant with us
  in Jesus Christ our Lord.

2 Step out in faith that he will be our God
  and we shall be his people:
      for the lost are restored,
      from the west to the east;
      we shall all know the Lord
      from the greatest to the least:
  and this is God's new covenant with us
  in Jesus Christ our Lord:

  And this is God's new covenant with us
  in Jesus Christ our Lord.

198
from Psalm 23
Christopher Idle

1 The Lord my shepherd rules my life
   and gives me all I need;
   he leads me by refreshing streams,
   in pastures green I feed.

2 The Lord revives my failing strength,
   he makes my joy complete;
   and in right paths, for his name's sake
   he guides my faltering feet.

3 Though in a valley dark as death,
   no evil makes me fear;
   your shepherd's staff protects my way,
   for you are with me there.

4 While all my enemies look on
   you spread a royal feast;
   you fill my cup, anoint my head,
   and treat me as your guest.

5 Your goodness and your gracious love
   pursue me all my days;
   your house, O Lord, shall be my home –
   your name, my endless praise.

6 To Father, Son and Spirit, praise!
   to God, whom we adore,
   be worship, glory, power and love,
   both now and evermore!

199 after Isaiah 6
H. W. Guiness

Version 1

Mine are the hands to do the work,
your servant I will be,
my lips shall sound the glorious news –
Lord, here am I, send me!

Version 2

Mine are the hands to do the work,
my feet shall run for thee,
my lips shall sound the glorious news –
Lord, here am I, send me!

200 after Isaiah 2
Unknown

O sinner man, where will you run to?
O sinner man, where will you run to?
O sinner man, where will you run to
all on that day?

1 Run to the rocks – 'Rocks won't you hide me?'
 run to the rocks – 'Rocks won't you hide me?'
 run to the rocks – 'Rocks won't you hide me?'
 all on that day:
  O sinner man...

2 Run to the sea – sea is a-boiling,
 run to the sea – sea is a-boiling,
 run to the sea – sea is a-boiling,
 all on that day:
  O sinner man...

3 Run to the Lord – 'Lord won't you hide me?'
 run to the Lord – 'Lord won't you hide me?'
 run to the Lord – 'Lord won't you hide me?'
 all on that day:
  O sinner man...

4 O sinner man, should been a-praying,
 O sinner man, should been a-praying,
 O sinner man, should been a-praying,
 all on that day:
  O sinner man...

201   Estelle White

1 O the love of my Lord is the essence
   of all that I love here on earth! –
       all the beauty I see
       he has given to me,
   and his giving is gentle as silence.

2 Every day, every hour, every moment
   have been blessed by the strength of his love:
       at the turn of each tide
       he is there at my side,
   and his touch is as gentle as silence.

3 There've been times when I've turned
       from his presence,
   and I've walked other paths, other ways:
       but I've called on his name
       in the dark of my shame,
   and his mercy was gentle as silence.

202

Unknown

1 O when the saints go marching in,
O when the saints go marching in;
I want to be in that number
when the saints go marching in!

2 O when they crown him Lord of all,
O when they crown him Lord of all;
I want to be in that number
when they crown him Lord of all.

3 O when all knees bow at his name,
O when all knees bow at his name;
I want to be in that number
when all knees bow at his name.

4 O when they sing the saviour's praise,
O when they sing the saviour's praise;
I want to be in that number
when they sing the saviour's praise.

5 O when the saints go marching in,
O when the saints go marching in;
I want to be in that number
when the saints go marching in!

JESUS PRAISE

203

Unknown

1 Peace is flowing like a river,
   flowing out through you and me,
   spreading out into the desert,
   setting all the captives free!
      Let it flow through me,
      let it flow through me,
      let the mighty love of God
      flow out through me!

      Let it flow through me,
      let it flow through me,
      let the mighty love of God
      flow out through me!

2 Joy is flowing like a river,
   flowing out through you and me,
   spreading out into the desert,
   setting all the captives free:
      Let it flow . . !

3 Love is flowing like a river,
   flowing out through you and me,
   spreading out into the desert,
   setting all the captives free:
      Let it flow . . !

4 Hope is flowing like a river,
   flowing out through you and me,
   spreading out into the desert,
   setting all the captives free:
      Let it flow . . !

204

Karen Lafferty

Seek ye first the kingdom of God
and his righteousness;
and all these things will be added unto you:
allelu, alleluia!

Alleluia,
alleluia,
alleluia,
alleluia!

Ask and it shall be given unto you,
seek and ye shall find;
knock and it shall be opened unto you:
allelu, alleluia!

Alleluia . . . !

The second verse is not part of the song as originally written. Its
origin is unknown.

205

Andrae Crouch

1 Soon and very soon we are going to see the King,
soon and very soon we are going to see the King,
soon and very soon we are going to see the King,
alleluia, alleluia, we're going to see the King!

2 No more crying there, we are going to see the King,
no more crying there, we are going to see the King,
no more crying there, we are going to see the King:
alleluia, alleluia, we're going to see the King!

3 No more dying there, we're going to see the King,
no more dying there, we're going to see the King,
no more dying there, we're going to see the King:
alleluia, alleluia, we're going to see the King
allcluia, allcluia, alleluia, alleluia.

4 Soon and very soon we are going to see the King,
soon and very soon we are going to see the King,
soon and very soon we are going to see the King,
alleluia, alleluia, we're going to see the King!
alleluia, alleluia, alleluia, alleluia.

THE CHRISTIAN LIFE

206 from Psalm 37, Lamentations 3 etc.
E. McNeill

The steadfast love of the Lord never ceases,
his mercies never come to an end;
they are new every morning, new every morning:
Great is your faithfulness, O Lord,
great is your faithfulness!

1 The Lord is my portion, says my soul,
therefore I will hope in him.
The steadfast love...

2 The Lord is good to those who wait for him,
to the soul that seeks him:
it is good that we should wait quietly
for the salvation of the Lord.
The steadfast love...

3 The Lord will not cast off for ever,
but will have compassion:
for he does not willingly afflict or
grieve the sons of men.
The steadfast love...

4 So let us examine all our ways,
and return to the Lord:
let us lift up our hearts and hands
to God in heaven.
The steadfast love...

207 after Genesis 8
Margaret Bowdler

1 The Summer has gone and the Autumn turns to gold,
  the Autumn turns to gold;
 the seasons go around and the year is growing old,
  the year is growing old:
 as long as Earth remains, seed time,
  harvest shall not fail,
  the harvest shall not fail.
 For God gave us a promise
  and God's word shall prevail
 and God's word shall prevail.

2 The years roll past and mortal man must die,
  and mortal man must die;
 for human flesh is frail and our life here soon goes by,
  and our life here soon goes by:
 beyond all time and space we shall live with our Lord
  and reign in heaven above,
  where life and joy and peace will remain
 and no more pain –
  a kingdom filled with love!

208 after Matthew 25, Song of Songs 2
Graham Kendrick

Tell me why do you weep?
Tell me why do you mourn?
Tell me why do you look so sad?
Tell me why don't you dance?
Tell me why don't you sing?
Tell me why don't you look to the sky?

1 Don't you know that your king is coming?
Don't you know that your king is nigh?
He is even at the gates of Jerusalem,
he is coming on the morning sky.
Tell me...

2 Don't you know that the feast is ready,
ready for the bride to come?
Brothers, keep your lamps a-burning –
the ending of the age is come.
Tell me...

3 Don't you know you are the Lord's invited?
Don't you know you are the chosen ones?
You in whom he has delighted
shall rise with Jesus when he comes.
Tell me...

4 Come arise, my love, my fairest daughter:
the winter and the rain are gone,
the flowers of summer are appearing,
the time of singing songs has come.
Tell me...

JESUS PRAISE

5 Don't you know that your king is coming?
   Don't you know that your king is nigh?
   He is even at the gates of Jerusalem,
   he is coming on the morning sky.

209   Rom. 7:1, Jude 2, Heb. 4:3, Col. 1:4, 1 Cor. 15
          Robert Stoodley

Thanks be to God who gives us the victory,
gives us the victory through our Lord Jesus Christ;
thanks be to God who gives us the victory,
gives us the victory through our Lord Jesus Christ!

1 He is able to keep us from falling
  and to set us free from sin;
  so let us each live up to our calling
  and commit our way to him:
      Thanks be to God..!

2 Jesus knows all about our temptations –
  he has had to bear them too;
  he will show us how to escape them,
  if we trust him he will lead us through:
      Thanks be to God..!

3 He has led us from the power of darkness
  to the kingdom of his blessed Son;
  so let us join in praise together
  and rejoice in what the Lord has done:
      Thanks be to God..!

4 Praise the Lord for sending Jesus
  to the Cross of Calvary:
  now he's risen, reigns in power
  and death is swallowed up in victory:
  Thanks be to God..!

210 Unknown

1 There's a world out there –
  the Lord calls you to listen,
  there's a world out there – don't you hear it cry?
  There's a world out there – won't you stop and listen;
  won't you listen, listen, listen, listen?

2 There's a world out there –
  don't you hear it crying?
  there's a world out there – don't you hear it sighing?
  There's a world out there – don't you hear it dying?
  won't you listen, listen, listen, listen?

3 There's a world out there –
  the Lord calls you to serve him,
  there's a world out there – don't you hear his call?
  There's a world out there – won't you go out for him;
  won't you listen, listen, listen, listen?

211 Unknown

1 This world is not my home –
I'm just a-passing through,
my treasures are laid up
somewhere beyond the blue:
the saviour beckons me
from heaven's open door,
and I can't feel at home
in this world any more.

O Lord, you know, I have no friend like you:
if heaven's not my home, then Lord what will I do?
The saviour beckons me from heaven's open door,
and I can't feel at home in this world any more!

2 They're all expecting me,
and that's one thing I know,
my saviour pardoned me,
now onward I must go:
I know he'll take me through
though I am weak and poor,
and I can't feel at home
in this world any more.
   O Lord, you know...

3 Just over in glory land
we'll live eternally,
the saints on every hand
are shouting victory:
their songs of sweetest praise
drift back from heaven's shore –
and I can't feel at home
in this world any more.
   O Lord, you know...

THE CHRISTIAN LIFE

212 Richard Bewes

1 Though the world has forsaken God,
  treads a different path, lives a different way,
  I walk the road that the saviour trod,
  and all may know I live under Jesus' sway.

  They are watching you, marking all you do,
  hearing the things you say:
  let them see the saviour as he shines in you,
  let his power control you every day!

2 Men will look at the life I lead,
  see the side I take, and the things I love;
  they judge my Lord by my every deed –
  Lord, set my affections on things above!
    They are watching you...

3 When assailed in temptation's hour,
  by besetting sins, by the fear of man,
  then I can know Jesus' mighty power,
  and become like him in his perfect plan.
    They are watching you...

4 Here on earth people walk in night;
  with no lamp to guide, they are dead in sin:
  I know the Lord who can give them light,
  I live, yet not I, but Christ within!
    They are watching you...

213 from Proverbs 3
Unknown

Trust in the Lord with all your heart
and lean not unto your own understanding:
in all your ways acknowledge him
and he shall direct your paths.

214 Timothy Dudley-Smith

1 As water to the thirsty,
   as beauty to the eyes,
   as strength that follows weakness,
   as truth instead of lies,
   as songtime and springtime
   and summertime to be,
        so is my Lord,
        my living Lord,
   so is my Lord to me.

2 Like calm in place of clamour,
   like peace that follows pain,
   like meeting after parting,
   like sunshine after rain,
   like moonlight and starlight
   and sunlight on the sea,
        so is my Lord,
        my living Lord,
   so is my Lord to me.

3 As sleep that follows fever,
    as gold instead of grey,
    as freedom after bondage,
    as sunrise to the day,
    as home to the traveller
    and all he longs to see,
        so is my Lord,
        my living Lord,
    so is my Lord to me.

215 Unknown

1 Were you there when they crucified my Lord?
    Were you there when they crucified my Lord?
    O .. sometimes it causes me to tremble,
        tremble, tremble:
    were you there when they crucified my Lord?

2 Were you there when they nailed him to the tree?
    Were you there when they nailed him to the tree?
    O .. sometimes it causes me to tremble,
        tremble, tremble:
    were you there when they nailed him to the tree?

3 Were you there when they pierced him in the side?
    Were you there when they pierced him in the side?
    O .. sometimes it causes me to tremble,
        tremble, tremble:
    were you there when they pierced him in the side?

4 Were you there when the sun refused to shine?
  Were you there when the sun refused to shine?
  O . . sometimes it causes me to tremble,
     tremble, tremble:
  were you there when the sun refused to shine?

5 Were you there when they laid him in the tomb?
  Were you there when they laid him in the tomb?
  O . . sometimes it causes me to tremble,
     tremble, tremble:
  were you there when they laid him in the tomb?

6 Were you there when he rose up from the dead?
  Were you there when he rose up from the dead?
  O . . sometimes I feel like shouting 'Glory,
     glory, glory!' –
  were you there when he rose up from the dead?

THE CHRISTIAN LIFE

216 Richard Bewes

1 Which way are you choosing, the narrow or broad? –
  you'll have to make up your mind!
  Just give up your own way and follow the Lord:
  why don't you make up your mind?
  He died, the stranger of Galilee
  to bring salvation to you and me;
  a strong companion you'll prove him to be –
  so won't you make up your mind?

2 Which crowd will you follow, the large or the small? –
  be sure to make up your mind!
  The cost is demanding, but hear Jesus call:
  then come and make up your mind.
  Your friends may shun you unthinkingly,
  but Christ gives power and liberty;
  to life with purpose you'll find the key,
  when once you make up your mind.

3 On which are you resting, the rock or the sand? –
  you'd better make up your mind!
  With Christ as foundation your building will stand:
  but have you made up your mind?
  Temptations and trials must come your way,
  the storms of judgement will rage one day:
  take Jesus and on him your confidence stay –
  don't wait, but make up your mind!

4 O what will you do with the saviour today? –
  he bids you make up your mind!
  Repent and accept him without delay,
  O sinner, make up your mind!
  Why stumble alone along the road?
  He'll sort your tangles, he'll take your load,
  and in your heart he will make his abode –
  it's time to make up your mind!

217   from Isaiah 55
        Unknown

You shall go out with joy, and be led forth with peace,
and the mountains and the hills
    shall break forth before you.
There'll be shouts of joy, and the trees of the field,
    shall clap, shall clap their hands.
And the trees of the field shall clap their hands,
and the trees of the field shall clap their hands,
and the trees of the field shall clap their hands –
and you'll go out with joy.

SCRIPTURE INDEX

FIRST LINE INDEX